'Freddie is a remarkable young man. I am proud to know him and am proud to commend both him and his honest, challenging and encouraging book to you.'

Mike Pilavachi, co-founder and leader of Soul Survivor

'I love Freddie's passion for each of us to know the transforming power and presence of Jesus. There's so much truth in his encouragement that we will find real freedom by looking less at ourselves and more at God, and that the more we seek God's kingdom, the more richness we will find in our own lives.'

Ali Martin, Soul Survivor

'We believe that this book truly conveys a message for the church today: to be "the hands and feet" of Jesus Christ in the world. We pray that, as you read this book, you will be convicted that the local church (you and me) is God's only plan; but also that you will be encouraged, that, empowered by the Holy Spirit, we can "go and make disciples of the nations". Together we can . . .'

Tich and Joan Smith, founders of LIV Village

'*The Selfish Gospel* provides a challenging call to change the lens through which we view the gospel and to see it for what it is: a life-changing, all-consuming call to follow Jesus wherever he leads. We all need to hear Freddie's encouragement to rise up and build God's kingdom and to stand against our "me"-centred culture; that is where we'll find true freedom.'

Andy Croft, Soul Survivor

D0928231

Freddie is an author and a practising doctor who lives in London with his wife, Becky. They attend St Alban's Fulham together. He is a regular speaker at Soul Survivor festivals and contributed to the *Soul Survivor Youth Bible* in 2014. Freddie blogs about issues such as discipleship, church growth and the challenge of practising his faith every day.

THE
SELFISH
GOSPEL

THE
SELFISH
GOSPEL

*Be transformed by
giving it all*

FREDDIE PIMM

INTER-VARSITY PRESS
36 Causton Street, London SW1P 4ST, England
Email: ivp@ivpbooks.com
Website: www.ivpbooks.com

First published 2017

British Library Cataloguing-in-Publication Data
A catalogue record for this book is available from the British Library.

ISBN: 978–1–78359–517–4
eBook ISBN: 978–1–78359–518–1

Set in Bembo 10.5/15pt
Typeset in Great Britain by CRB Associates, Potterhanworth, Lincolnshire
Printed in Great Britain by Ashford Colour Press Ltd, Gosport, Hampshire

Inter-Varsity Press publishes Christian books that are true to the Bible and that communicate the gospel, develop discipleship and strengthen the church for its mission in the world.

IVP originated within the Inter-Varsity Fellowship, now the Universities and Colleges Christian Fellowship, a student movement connecting Christian Unions in universities and colleges throughout Great Britain, and a member movement of the International Fellowship of Evangelical Students. Website: www.uccf.org.uk. That historic association is maintained, and all senior IVP staff and committee members subscribe to the UCCF Basis of Faith.

Contents

Foreword

I have known Freddie Pimm since he was a teenager. I have watched him face many of the discipleship issues he talks about in this book; first as a schoolboy, then in the years studying medicine at university and now as a young doctor. He is not a well-known Christian leader and has no formal theological training. So why should you read this book? Because it is both wise and authentic. And this is because Freddie himself is both wise and authentic. He has not written from a remote ivory tower. This is not theory; it is rooted in life.

The Selfish Gospel is a book that invites us to more. Freddie holds up a mirror to the 'me-centred' culture that has permeated the whole of society and challenges us to live sacrificially in pursuit of furthering God's kingdom. Through his medical lens, Freddie studies the symptoms, diagnosis and treatment of the church, leading us towards a gospel that offers freedom for us and transformation for the world around us.

This book is a timely reminder that we can't preach the gospel that Jesus died for us and that we can receive his forgiveness, and then end the good news there. That is a diluted gospel. It may seem more palatable if it requires no response, but it doesn't tell the full story or draw us into a life of discipleship and relationship with God. Following Jesus comes at a cost, but the riches we gain far outweigh anything we can give.

What stands out in this book is Freddie's passion for Jesus and the church. Freddie talks to us from a place of honesty about his own struggles in this journey as he's tried to work out what it means to follow Jesus. There's no finger-pointing, just a clear desire to see God's church be all that it can be. I have seen around the world that the places where the church thrives the most are where followers of Jesus step beyond the church walls and engage with their community. Churches that live most outwardly to usher in God's kingdom tend to be the places of the greatest growth and life.

Throughout *The Selfish Gospel*, Freddie steers clear of legalism or the idea that we can earn our salvation. He continually points us back to Jesus, reminding us that we don't earn God's love, we embrace it and respond accordingly. As we let go of our selfish lives, we embrace a much richer gospel; we find a much truer picture of what it means to follow Jesus and to build his kingdom.

Freddie is a remarkable young man. I am proud to know him and am proud to commend both him and his honest, challenging and encouraging book to you.

Mike Pilavachi, co-founder and leader of Soul Survivor

Acknowledgments

I am acutely aware that this book has only been made possible because of the investment, support and opportunity that have been offered to me. I thank God for all those people who have helped this book on its journey from a collection of ideas swirling round in my head to published manuscript. The truth is that I have been blessed by many friends and mentors throughout my life, and they have all fed into and nurtured these thoughts and ideas as they developed in me.

I am only in this position today because of the opportunities that have been given to me and the faith that has been shown me. So to begin, I want to thank everyone who has prayed for me, encouraged me, invested in me and taught me over the years. This book has been a lifetime in the making and, more than anything, it is the product of all those who have blessed me.

I must extend special thanks to Mike and his team at Soul Survivor, who first kindled my passion for teaching and provided it space to grow and develop. Mike is a true friend and I will be eternally grateful for the remarkable risk he took when he first invited me to speak at Momentum Festival in the summer of 2011.

Second, I must thank my mum and dad. They have sacrificed so much for me, and anything that I have achieved is only because of all that they have given me. I am very blessed to have parents who have so gracefully provided for and encouraged me throughout my life.

I would also like to thank my wife, Becky. On a human level, it is Becky who has supported and nurtured me (and this book) over the last two years! But more than that, on a practical level, it was Becky who first put me in touch with the publisher — so this book would never have been possible without her talent and skill. I would be entirely lost without Becky's strength and guidance.

And this of course leads me to thank Elizabeth and the team at IVP. The greatest gift they have given me is in taking a chance on this book and giving it life; there are many who would not have been so bold. Furthermore, it is their incredible efforts that have taken it from a scratchy, rough draft to a polished and finished product.

To all of those who have played a part in the development of this book, I hope the finished product is something you can each be proud of.

Author's note

To protect the anonymity of those mentioned in this book, any discussions involving patients whom I have previously encountered in my medical practice have been subject to changes of minor details such as names, genders, dates, timing and order of events. While the spirit and nature of these stories has remained true, the essential details have had to change so that patients cannot be recognized through the narrative of the stories that I have shared.

The Selfish Gospel

A message of love and forgiveness that doesn't interfere with our lives.

- ☑ Loved?
- ☑ Forgiven?
- ☒ Builder of God's kingdom?

Introduction

I have these 'gulp' moments as a junior doctor. My day is happily ticking along, everything is under control. I'm well within my comfort zone. Then BAM! I'm thrown into a desperate situation that tests me to my limits, and I never even saw it coming. I'm driven so far out of my comfort zone that I can barely see it in the rear-view mirror. Suddenly, I am overcome by the desperate nature of the situation. And yet, despite the dread eating away at my confidence, I am forced to take a big gulp and press on, because to stop or to go back would be a hundred times worse.

There was the girl who came to my clinic the day after her father had committed suicide. She was in floods of tears as she tried to explain the flurry of emotion this had caused her family. That was a big gulp moment. How was I supposed to speak any hope into her situation?

Then there was the patient I was called to visit in the middle of the night. He had been very unwell for a long time, but had taken a sudden and severe turn for the worse. As I arrived and started to assess him, he looked like his heart might stop at any moment. His wife knelt on the floor beside him, clutching his hand, begging us to keep him alive for the sake of their seven-year-old son. Another big gulp. How could I bring hope to that situation?

The reason I'm telling you about these 'gulp' moments is because I'm worried that this, the book you are holding in your hands, may be one of those moments too. My name is Freddie Pimm and I am a junior doctor living and practising in London. I'm also a Christian, and the book you are holding is a brief look at the symptoms, diagnosis and treatment of one of the most complex patients I have ever encountered: the body of Christ, the church.

You see, I believe that in many areas of the church today, we are not as healthy as we ought to be. In some areas we are thriving; there is new life, new growth. There are people coming into contact with God and coming away changed, their lives transformed. Here, the church is seeing transformation – of ourselves, our communities and our nation. This is the picture of the church that Jesus calls us to see. This is Jesus' picture of health. In other areas of the church, however, we are failing to exert the same transformative power.

In January 2016, the *Daily Telegraph* published an article under the headline 'Church of England Attendances Plunge to Record Low'.[1] Although in some areas of the church we are seeing the most amazing things happen, headlines like this seem to suggest something different. They show a picture of the church deteriorating, gradually losing our strength until we give up and breathe our last. You cannot believe everything you read in the media, but the fact that this headline exists at all would suggest that we are having a very real struggle with transformation in the church.

Whether you feel it in the church you attend or in the communities of which you are a part, it is hard to deny that some areas of the church are unwell. And, if the amazing pockets of transformation that some churches are seeing are lost in a sea of conformity and decline, the status of our patient – the church – becomes even more critical indeed.

But what's that got to do with you and me?

If you are reading this at a buzzing summer festival, discussing it with your inspiring home group or waiting for your vibrant church service to start – praise Jesus! You are reading this in a pocket of transformation. You are reading this in a pocket of health! However, if your life is anything like mine, it won't take long for you to think of a place where being a Christian is counter-cultural, controversial and straight-up hard work. The Bible says the church is the body of Christ – and it's a body with many parts. So if some parts are unwell, it is as much a problem for those who are thriving as it is for the ones just surviving.

And this is why this is a big 'gulp' moment for me: I am a relatively normal Christian guy with a relatively normal Christian story. I have a relatively normal job and I attend a relatively normal church in a relatively normal part of the country. If you want two words to sum me up, 'relatively normal' would do it! And so this is a big 'gulp' moment because I am going to try to write openly and vulnerably about issues that I feel most keenly in my life and at the churches I have attended. This is a big 'gulp' moment because, at its heart, this book is a critique of myself as much as it is a critique of our church.

And so, before we go any further, I probably need to ask for your forgiveness. Forgive me for my hypocritical nature. Forgive me if I seem brutal or harsh in my assessment of the state of the modern church. Forgive me if you feel that I am attacking you or your way of doing church as I highlight these problems. I really don't mean to. But the thing about these 'gulp' moments is that, even though the problem may seem big and the prognosis bleak, we have to swallow all of that apprehension and fear and press on, because to stop or go back would be a hundred times worse.

BUT WHO AM I TO SAY?

Let me tell you a bit more about me and my (relatively normal) life. Bear with me, because if you understand where I'm coming from and the journey I've been on, perhaps you will start to understand the perspective I have and how that has led me to make these observations – observations I'm sure many of you will have made as well.

I grew up in a quiet seaside town called Weston-Super-Mare; I was three years old when my parents did an Alpha course at a church they attended from time to time. Here they encountered the Holy Spirit in a tangible way. That was it for us; there was no way back. And so for as long as I can remember, I have called myself a Christian.

From the age of three I attended St Paul's Weston-Super-Mare. It's a fantastic church. However, as I'm sure you are aware, being brought up in a church doesn't necessarily make someone a Christian! Actually, the moment that Christianity really made sense for me was at a summer camp called New Wine. There, at the age of ten, I began to realize that being a Christian meant having a *relationship* with Jesus. As a level-headed ten-year-old, I knew I was a Christian, and so, putting two and two together, I realized that this meant that I had to start having this relationship with Jesus.

From there, I grew up as a Christian in the church. During my adolescent years I attended youth groups and summer festivals. I had times where the focus of my entire being was on being a Christian, and other times where I was more concerned with fitting in with the crowd or chasing girls.

As I grew more serious about my faith I began the process of discipleship, being transformed through spiritual discipline. It would often be in fits and starts, usually after a summer festival or a church conference. I would get excited and passionate, and so for a few short weeks I would eagerly read my Bible and pray every evening. After these few weeks, the passion would fizzle out and I'd leave discipleship behind for a while. And yet, as the years went by and I matured and became more disciplined in myself, I gradually learned the pleasure to be gained from spiritual discipline and discipleship.

What could possibly go wrong?

Well, university happened. When I went to university in London, a mixture of girls, alcohol and failure to really root myself in a church led me to walk away from my faith. Although I continued to refer to myself as a Christian, I indulged the stereotypical student lifestyle until I got so far away from my faith that one day I looked back at it and decided it wasn't for me. I thought to myself, 'If God exists, if he actually cares about the way I'm living, then he can come and find me, but I'm not convinced he exists and I'm not convinced he cares.'

Well, it turns out God did care – not in a disgruntled, vengeful way, but as a father cares for his son. Towards the end of my first year, through a good friend, God called me back into relationship with him. It took a year or so to break off the bad habits I'd developed in my first year, but certainly by the beginning of my third year of university, I was very serious about my faith again.

It was around this time that I also began attending St Albans Fulham. Not only was this church newly planted from an amazing London church called Holy Trinity Brompton (HTB), but it was also just down the road from me – very convenient for a uni student! The vicar – an amazing man called Matt Hogg – had a vision to build a community intent on bringing God's kingdom to our area. It struck a chord with me, and six years later, after medical school, two degrees and several years of training, I'm still a member of St Albans. Which brings us back to the present and back to this book.

WHERE IS OUR TRANSFORMATIVE INFLUENCE?

Over the last fifty years, the church's influence in UK society has certainly diminished. Its reputation has been badly tarnished and it has seen a huge decline in attendances, although a small recovery is now beginning in some areas, such as the church as a whole in London[2] or the Fresh Expressions movement within the Church of England.[3]

This mixed picture of the church is a far cry from the will of Jesus. He came heralding a revolution, the release of grace and mercy, and a profound shift in the values that people hold dear. Jesus came preaching transformation and he achieved it, with the early church continuing his work in an incredible way. And so our present situation makes me question: why is it that some parts of the church are thriving while others are in decline? Why do many areas of the church today seem to be lacking this transformative influence that Jesus had in abundance? And if the church is the people, what does this say about us as individuals?

Every church has people who can tell you stories of the most amazing miracles they've seen. You know the kind of stories I mean. There's a Christian, they're on a plane (for some reason these things always happen on planes) and they manage to lead their entire row of passengers to Christ in the space of a few short hours – both sides of the aisle!

Like any Christian, I hear these stories and I buzz with excitement. But then I look at myself in the mirror and I'm faced with an uncomfortable question: how much have I been transformed in the last year? How well am I transforming the world around me? Some Christians may lead whole rows of people to faith, but many of us haven't seen that amazing transformational power in the same way.

Are some Christians somehow more powerful than the rest of us? Is it because they have been blessed with a different Holy Spirit? Absolutely not! We are all members of the same church. We all believe in the same Jesus and he promised us all that same Holy

Spirit. We may be 2,000 years down the line, but the passing millennia have not changed our unchanging God or the blessing of his Holy Spirit. Jesus' gospel is no less powerful today than it was all those years ago. And so why does so much of society see the gospel as outdated, boring or irrelevant?

BUT IS THE GOSPEL REALLY THAT IRRELEVANT?

The truth is, today more than ever, our society is crying out for integrity and authenticity in relationships. Everybody wants to be loved sacrificially, in a way that is committed and real, but few can find that sacrificial love. That love is a core component of our gospel message and yet, in spite of this, as a church we are failing to see widespread transformation. And so my question about the church as a whole becomes uncomfortably a question about me. Why don't I see that transformative power in my life and the lives of so many around me?

Well, I've chewed on this question, and others like it, for quite some time. These questions sometimes seem too big to handle. But I've decided to start in the only way I know how: by taking a look at the symptoms. In the areas where we are struggling to have a transformative influence, I believe many of us will have seen the following symptoms:

1   Christians who have forgotten what it means to be disciples.
2   Christians who are inwardly focused.
3   Christians who have been seen as unattractive by society.

Now, if you came into a doctor's clinic with a sore throat, cough and a runny nose, you wouldn't be told that each of those complaints is an isolated disease in its own right. Each of those problems is a symptom of an underlying illness – a cold. In the same way, I would suggest that each of the problems listed above is a symptom of an underlying condition: our narrowed, too often (*gulp*) selfish understanding of the gospel.

Just as with any medical illness, it is only when we have a proper understanding of the symptoms that we gain a proper understanding of the underlying cause. And it is only when we gain this proper understanding of the underlying cause that we can seek to make it better. That's exactly what I am going to try to do in this book. Taking each of the 'symptoms' in turn, I want us to look at how they affect our church's ability to transform and where they cause problems. Then, turning to the 'diagnosis', I want to take a deeper look at the Selfish Gospel that many of us, myself included, have too often come to understand. Once we have unpacked and begun to understand the problems caused by the Selfish Gospel, we can explore how we can start to mend it. And, far from being hopeless, Jesus' gospel, embraced in its entirety, provides us with the 'cure'.

By addressing the Selfish Gospel head on, we will be able to reboot our transformative edge to full health. And, when we do, our lives, our churches and our wider communities will never be the same again.

The symptoms

- ☐ Delirious disciples
- ☐ Locked-in syndrome
- ☐ The Elephant Man

1 The symptoms
Delirious disciples

THE FESTIVAL FLATLINE

Standing in the crowd at Soul Survivor's summer festival, I felt empty-handed and broken. I was so profoundly aware of my numerous failings and God's awesome grace.

The previous year hadn't gone as planned. I could remember all too clearly how, in the weeks following last year's festival, I'd gradually lost the fire and the passion I'd felt. Now, standing muddy and undone in that Big Top tent, I realized that I'd wandered away from this feeling until my faith had become something that I'd only half-heartedly engage with on a Sunday. I knew Jesus wanted more of me.

And so, as I sang those lyrics, I recommitted my life to Christ. It was the same thing I'd done the previous year, but that didn't matter. I told God that this year would be different. And it was: returning to 'real life' with renewed drive and passion, I prayed and read the Bible, and surrounded myself with the worship of the week we'd just had. It was great. At least, it was for three weeks. But then, I got that new computer game . . . and joined that new rugby club . . . oh, and fell for that girl . . .

As someone who has been brought up in the church, I've seen this post-festival pattern play out time and time again. Between the ages of thirteen and seventeen, I would go to a big Christian conference, and while I was there I would get really passionate about God. I would go home resolving to change my ways – to shake bad habits and take on some godly ones instead. I told God I'd pray more, I told him I would study my Bible and meditate. I meant those vows with everything that I had.

But each and every time, the 'festival buzz' would fade, and my well-meaning commitments would soon be forgotten. My spiritual growth would falter. I'd flatline for months at a time until I had a particularly powerful worship session or attended another festival. There I'd see a jump in passion levels and develop a renewed commitment to prayer, and I'd slowly start to become spiritually healthy again.

IT'S AN EPIDEMIC

I pray my festival flatlining was the exception to the rule. But my experience growing up in the church leads me to believe this might not be the case. I was at church and youth group more or less every week. Every year I would go to two or three Christian festivals. But in that time, no-one explained to me *why* I was supposed to be reading the Bible and praying. No-one really modelled the process of discipleship to me. No-one modelled how to eliminate the festival flatline and take responsibility for my own spiritual growth. And I speak to people every week who have that same problem, people who are not engaged in a process of discipleship.

One of my best friends once told me about a conversation he'd had with the long-standing youth worship leader at his church. They were talking about spiritual discipline and personal devotional times – time spent with God in prayer, reading the Bible, meditating and so on. This worship leader was trying to convince my friend that he was wrong to promote the importance of spiritual discipline, to promote regular times of prayer and reading the Bible, because it made people who struggle with those things, such as himself, feel guilty.

Now, on the one hand I take this worship leader's point. The danger of focusing on spiritual discipline is that it comes across as a guilt trip; it becomes just another sermon about how we need to pray and read our Bibles more. And yes, many people can struggle with spiritual discipline; that's why it's called discipline! But it's not just about doing those things for the sake of it. It's about doing those things *in order* to know God's heart and be transformed by his Holy Spirit. Just because something may be difficult doesn't mean it's not important. Can you imagine if I were to stop telling all my patients to quit smoking because it might be difficult for them? While it may be a difficult process at first, the benefits of quitting smoking are huge – and the same is true of spiritual discipline.

What breaks my heart is that this story, as far as I can see, is not an isolated episode. Time and time again, I speak to Christians who say they don't have a regular time of prayer, don't read the Bible and don't engage in a process designed to grow them spiritually. And that's not because we've become 'bad Christians'; the church isn't suddenly full of rebels or backsliders! It seems to me that we've reached this point because too often we don't have a culture of discipleship in our churches.

It's like we've become a bit delirious . . .

DELIRIOUS DISCIPLES

What does the word 'delirious' mean to you? Like me, you may remember the band Delirious?, led by a guy called Martin Smith. They rocked Christian culture between 1997 and 2009. I went to a Delirious? gig in 2003, and at that point it felt like the coolest thing I'd ever done with my life. A lot of people use the word to mean an inflated sense of happiness. You know, 'I'm so happy about the football! I'm delirious!' So maybe being delirious is a good thing to you.

But I'm afraid that within the medical world, being delirious is most definitely a bad thing. Delirium (the state of being delirious) is an old-fashioned medical term for what we now call 'acute confusional state'. When you're delirious, or in this acute confusional state, you forget who you are, where you are, what time it is – even what you're doing in that place. People get this way when they are profoundly unwell in hospital; it's very common among the elderly when they're admitted. My fear is that, like those elderly patients, at times, many of us have become a bit delirious as Christians.

I once walked into an elderly patient's room and he turned, looked me in the eye and remarked, 'We're in a marmalade factory.' There was no hint of humour on his face.

I stopped, slightly taken aback, and asked him, 'If we're in a marmalade factory, who am I?'

He replied matter-of-factly, 'You're a marmalade factory worker; you make the marmalade around here.'

I've been accused of many things in my life, but never before had I been called a marmalade factory worker. The thing is, there was a grain of truth in what he said: he'd just had marmalade on toast for breakfast! In the same way, I think many of us have forgotten what it means to be a disciple of Christ. We may have a few scattered grains of truth rooted deep in our memories, but we seem to have missed the bigger picture. We've got a bit confused, and somehow lost our way.

'Go and make disciples of all nations, baptising them in the name of the Father and of the Son and of the Holy Spirit, and teaching them to obey everything I have commanded you,' said Jesus in his final instructions to the church in Matthew 28:19–20.

For many of us, 'being a Christian' is about putting our faith in Jesus, being baptized in the Holy Spirit, loving God and loving our neighbour as ourselves. And there is far more than a grain of truth in each of these things. But Jesus is pretty clear in his last words to the church that our mission statement is to make disciples. We need to make disciples. And yet, in our state of delirium, many of us seem to have forgotten those words.

Mike Breen, in his book *Building a Discipling Culture*, makes the point that, as a church, we can often understand Jesus' statement to mean: 'Go and get everyone you can to join your church.' Although obviously there is quite a big dollop of marmalade-truth in that, Jesus' call to action also addresses those people who are already in our churches. Just because I regularly attend services doesn't make me a disciple.[4] But sometimes we focus so much on that first aspect of filling the pews that we neglect the second aspect of Jesus' command. The danger is, if we neglect the second part, then we grow people with faith in Christ but we do not grow disciples.

Discipleship rarely happens by accident. It almost always takes a conscious effort. A friend recently told me a story about a young man from an unchurched background who came to faith while at their church. Having committed his life to Christ, this young man became an active member of the church community, making friends and generally getting involved. He slowly began to serve with the church worship team. One evening, about a year after giving his life to Christ, the worship team were discussing their personal prayer lives and the importance of having regular devotional times. At the end of the worship session, my friend told me how this young man came up to him and asked him, 'What's a devotional time? I've never heard of that before.' It seemed that despite getting very involved with this church, over the space of a year no-one had explained to him what it meant to seek God in his personal time, let alone emphasized the importance of it. As I listened to my friend's story, all I could do was sympathize. It's pretty hard to stumble into a routine of devotional time or a process of discipleship if no-one has ever shown you how to do it.

SHAKING OFF THE DELIRIUM

When I was sixteen, I read a book that directly challenged my pattern of 'festival flatlining' that I told you about at the start of this chapter. It was called *The Pursuit of God* by A. W. Tozer.[5] In this book, Tozer suggests that the human heart is made to pursue God above all other desires, but as fallen beings we often take other things like possessions or relationships into our hearts, and they get between us and God. As I read that, my sixteen-year-old self had his mind blown. Tozer knew what he was talking about!

Suddenly I realized why I would lose my focus on God after a conference or festival. Initially I would be pursuing God before everything else, but then I would get distracted by something (usually computer games or girls . . . are you sensing a theme?) and suddenly that would be the thing that I was pursuing first. Without God as my priority pursuit, I'd lose that focus on God and consequently my motivation to pray and study the Bible. Like a distant friend you haven't bothered to see in a while, the thought of hanging out with God became more and more like hard work the longer I put it off. My first pursuit, on the other hand, would take God's place and become almost irresistible.

So around the age of sixteen, I started to grasp why I kept failing to maintain my festival focus. But still, no-one was really explaining to me why I should *want* to. As a Christian, I knew I was 'supposed' to pray, but I was struggling to find people telling me why or modelling how. It's not that there weren't any Christians doing this stuff in my church. But there were few to whom I could relate. Within my generation at the church, it was only the 'super-spiritual' Christians who would do this stuff. Culturally, it was very normal for us not to have those regular times of prayer or study.

It was a year or so later when I first read *A Celebration of Discipline* by Richard Foster – another amazing author – that I suddenly understood why I should read the Bible and pray. Foster describes twelve 'spiritual disciplines' which we should engage with as part of our discipleship. First there are the personal disciplines of praying, studying Scripture, meditation and fasting. Then come the corporate disciplines of confession, worship, guidance and cele-bration. And finally there are the outward disciplines of simplicity, solitude, submission and service.[6] More importantly, Foster also explains why each of these is important. At the beginning of his book, he uses an analogy:

> A farmer is helpless to grow grain; all he can do is provide the right conditions for the growth of grain. He cultivates the ground, plants the seed, he waters the plants, and then the nat-ural forces of the earth take over and up comes the grain. This is the way it is with the spiritual disciplines – they are a way of sowing to the spirit. The Disciplines are God's way of getting us into the ground; they put us where he can work within us and transform us.[7]

Suddenly this word 'discipleship' had a true meaning to me. I'd been using the word for as long as I could remember, but now it dawned on me what discipleship truly was. Discipleship isn't about praying to tick some spiritual box every day or studying the Bible so that we understand theological doctrines and theories. The

Greek word for 'disciple' literally means learner. Discipleship is about investing in our relationship with God and learning so that we become more like him. At its core, discipleship is the process of being transformed into the person that Jesus would be if he were you. That's what it meant for first-century Jews – for Jesus' first disciples. For Peter, James, John and the rest, discipleship was about learning to imitate Jesus: how your rabbi treated others was how you treated others.[8] How your rabbi prayed and studied the scriptures was how you prayed and studied the scriptures. How your rabbi ate his dinner was how you ate your dinner. The imitation was intended to be that close. That's what being a disciple is all about: engaging with the spiritual disciplines daily, constantly reflecting on our experiences and trying to work out how we can become more Christ-like, then relying on the Holy Spirit to transform us.

A CULTURE OF DISCIPLESHIP?

I think this is where the problem starts to come in for many of us. Nobody expects someone to give their life to Christ and instantly grow into a mature Christian; we need to be trained in this stuff! But we don't seem to build a culture that encourages that training. It's as though once a person admits their need for Jesus and gives their life to God (sometimes called a 'sinner's prayer'), then we've done the hard part. Mission accomplished! We may give him or her a 'new believers' pack – which can be a very helpful tool – but for the most part we just hope that he or she picks up the rest along the way.

Culture sets the tone for action. At university, I was a member of the medical school rugby club and we had a very interesting culture around training. I spent a lot of time playing for the third team. We were the social heart of the club, but I wouldn't have said we were great rugby players. You wouldn't catch us at training on a Monday or Thursday, but we'd turn up for matches on a Wednesday and lead the social gathering afterwards. All right, so 'not great' was an understatement. We were awful at rugby! We never trained and we had no continuity of selection because people would be dropping in and out of the team at a moment's notice. I may remember the parties, but I don't remember winning all that much.

But the first team were different. They knew that if you didn't train, you didn't play. They trained twice a week, and did weights and fitness on their days off. They had a culture where it was abnormal if you weren't at training. If you were a member of the third team, it was abnormal if you were!

There is a reason why one of those two teams won most of the competitions it entered, while the other team got relegated twice in two years. No prizes for guessing which was which! My fear is that, as a church, we are more like the third team than the first team when it comes to discipleship.

It's a bit like this: the average contemporary church focuses on the Sunday service. These events are the heart of the church and tend to centre on worship and teaching. Many church members will be encouraged to serve at these services, welcoming new people, serving coffee and leading prayers, worship or teaching.

There will also be a variety of church events throughout the week. There will probably be home groups, youth groups and student groups. There will probably be a prayer meeting or a course for people exploring faith, a course for married people or a course for parents. The church may also have a social justice arm, perhaps working with the local foodbank or meeting another need in their community. But very rarely do we make time in our church schedules to promote discipleship. We may have the odd sermon on the topic, but too often we don't have structures in place to grow a culture of discipleship. Instead, the focus of spiritual growth comes from the Sunday service. But as we know, Jesus did not commission us to have great Sunday services; he commissioned us to make disciples.

If our purpose as Christians is to be transformed into Jesus' likeness through a process of discipleship, by the power of the Holy Spirit, that means that we need to be able to have intimate encounters with the Holy Spirit wherever we are – whether we are home alone, out in the beauty of creation or surrounded by thousands of others at a summer festival. But without a culture of discipleship encouraging us to take ownership of our day-to-day disciple-ship, our spiritual growth becomes dependent on outside sources. Our spiritual transformation may come from hearing a powerful word from the preacher, or having a particularly intimate time of worship – and there's nothing wrong with meeting God in these ways. However, if all our encounters with Jesus happen in church on Sundays, then we are reliant on being spoon-fed.

Picture a parent with a young child. The child is five, but however hard the parents have tried, they can't get the infant to take control of her meals and start to feed herself. The child will only eat if the parents stand there and shovel food into her mouth. Now, if that child were brought to see me as a doctor in clinic, I would start to worry that there was something seriously wrong with her development. Now replace the words 'parent' with 'leader', 'child' with 'Christian' and 'food' with 'spiritual growth'. That situation, where we are not able to take responsibility for our own spiritual growth, should set alarm bells ringing in the church. We may have a wonderful 'Hub' or 'Small Group' to spur us on midweek, but as we know, discipleship is much more than a weekly event. It is a daily routine and lifestyle that has to be consciously taught and modelled, usually with strong accountability structures.

It seems to me that, much like my third team and their culture of not training, too often in our church there is a culture that makes little space for discipleship despite it being central to what Jesus called us to be. Too often, we have a culture where transformation is centred on spoon-fed spirituality at large-scale church events.

BUT WHY DOES THIS MATTER?

Imagine you are given a canvas and a set of twelve paints, and are told to paint a landscape. You would be at a severe disadvantage if you chose to use only two colours – chances are, the painting would look odd or unbalanced. But in effect that is what we do if we only rely on the spiritual disciplines of corporate praise and teaching during our Sunday services. We become unbalanced.

If we do not learn to be responsible for our own growth and transformation, if we struggle to encounter the tangible power of the Holy Spirit outside of Sundays, then every Sunday we'll be going to church looking for that encounter. Just like teenage me, if we rely solely on our leaders for our spiritual growth, we will end up hitting the big festival highs, then losing the passion and focus throughout the year as 'real life' sets in and those awesome summer encounters fade away. Until next year's festivals, of course.

The truth is, at some point we need to go to our church services prepared to serve others and help them grow as they meet with the Holy Spirit, rather than going to church and looking for that encounter for ourselves. If everyone is heading to church hoping to receive and no-one is there prepared to serve, no wonder so many church leaders face burnout. If you use only two colours to paint your landscape, you should not be surprised if those colours run out rather quickly!

CONCLUSION

So far, we have seen that discipleship was a central aspect of Jesus' ministry (Matthew 28:19). We've also examined how true disciple-ship means learning to be an imitator of Jesus. However, despite this, discipleship can too often appear an alien process to many of us and it is all too common to find a culture where it is normal not to engage with many of the spiritual disciplines on a personal level.

We've looked at how this can make us too reliant on spoon-feeding for spiritual transformation and how this can lead to unbalanced congregations where the burden of spiritual development is placed on the shoulders of a few leaders. In this way, some of ourselves and our churches look a bit unwell. But don't worry – as we'll see later, Jesus never leaves us without the cure.

2 The symptoms
Locked-in syndrome

I had a friend who used to drive past a church on his way into school every morning. The church had this great billboard at the front, facing a busy road. Every week, without fail, the church would change the sign on the billboard. The signs were always on fluorescent paper and would have bold, capitalized letters screaming an evangelistic message usually along the lines of: 'One WEEK without prayer makes one WEAK' – or something similarly punny. My friend used to come into school on a Monday and share these slogans with the whole class during morning registration.

I loved those billboards! (By the way, did I ever tell you how cool I was at school?) But as I look back, I think they characterize a problem we have in the church. Personally I'm a big fan of puns, but to my mind, and I imagine yours also, a billboard message as a means of evangelism is just not going to cut it.

It's like the church has developed 'locked-in syndrome'. This is a condition where you receive damage to a specific part of the brainstem, often from a stroke, and it leaves your entire body and facial muscles paralysed, but your consciousness fully intact. The inside of your body functions normally, and you are completely aware and awake. At the same time, you're fully paralysed and cannot interact with the outside world at all. Some people can still move all or part of their eyes (or eyelids), but otherwise they're completely unable to communicate with anyone outside of themselves.

When we try to evangelize through a billboard, it's like we've developed locked-in syndrome – we're trapped in the church building and our only means of evangelism is through flickering an eyelid at the outside world. Within the church we are functioning completely normally, and everything goes along as it should do; we have our services, we run our home groups, we all talk about growth in the church. But when it comes to actually getting outside of the church community and talking to people who aren't members of the church family, we really struggle to get moving. We can put up a billboard, but otherwise we seem completely paralysed.

If a single billboard is how we expect to interact with the outside world, there's a lot of pressure on that one message. We're expecting people to drive past that billboard, read the message, feel convicted of sin, feel a desire to change, decide that this church is the best place to do that and take the billboard as an invite to attend the next Sunday service! It may be a great pun, but it might be a bit much expecting one poster to do all that.

Now I don't know what other evangelistic operations happened at this church and I don't mean to single it out – I never visited it myself, I only ever heard about it. But for me, that billboard is typical of a locked-in church culture paralysed in its efforts to interact with people who aren't yet Christians. 'Go outside of the church walls, Freddie? That's ridiculous! A few good billboards out the front, those will get the masses in.' The approach sounds simple, but I'm not sure it would prove that effective in practice.

I've never been to a church that wouldn't welcome growth. As Christians, many of us will talk about seeing the church flourish and the nation transformed. Almost every church leader will touch on evangelism in some way during the course of their ministry. I can't think of a church that I have visited that didn't have a strategy or a plan about how the church hopes to grow. But although we may talk a good game, I have to ask myself: how often do I go out of my way to welcome new faces at church? And not just part of the five-minute welcome wall. How often do I regularly engage in social activities outside of the church and the church family? How many of my close friends aren't Christians?

We may want growth, but in reality, for many of us it's like we're locked inside the church body, completely unable to communicate with those people who aren't already inside. And this is a sure-fire way to stunt transformation. Without interaction with society at large, how can we expect our faith to rub off on anyone new?

THE SUFFOCATING CHURCH CALENDAR

Having grown up in church, I think the most dangerous manifestation of this locked-in syndrome is the way that church life can often be structured. Too often, the church calendar can be organized so as to dominate the lives of its participants completely.

In the previous chapter, I talked about the attitude to training within my student rugby club – at university, that club was a big part of my life. In my third year it became an even bigger part, as I was voted in as the secretary of the club. At the same time, I was getting involved in church and really becoming passionate about my faith again. Both were great ways to spend my time, but what I noticed while working with the rugby club and investing heavily in the church concerned me.

The rugby club, by its nature, is an inwardly focused community. The purpose of the rugby club is to produce the best-quality team it can, so that they win as many trophies at as high a standard as possible. The church, by its own mission statement, is supposed to be an outwardly focused venture: the church exists to 'make disciples of all nations'. But what I noticed was that the daily life of the church looked remarkably similar to the daily life of the rugby club.

The rugby club had a few main events every week: match days on Wednesday and Saturday, training on Mondays and Thursdays, often with a number of rugby club members doing something social on a Friday. Through this weekly calendar, the rugby club dominates the lives of club members – at university I could easily find myself doing rugby events every day if I allowed it. And so, especially during my first couple of years, the rugby club took up the vast majority of my free time. Now, for an inwardly focused club, which finds its mission in growing the best team it possibly can from within the club community, that isn't the biggest issue.

But compare it to the church. We have our match days (Sunday services), training sessions (home groups) and, just like the rugby club, we also have social commitments with our friends from within the church. Unless we are very careful, we can easily manage to fill our weeks with church events: prayer meetings, Alpha courses to help on, youth and student groups to run and participate in, parenting or marriage courses, worship band practice, child protection training sessions . . . the list goes on.

Just as the rugby club – an admittedly inwardly focused institution – can dominate the life of its participants, so can the church. But unlike the rugby club, the church is supposed to exist for the benefit of its non-members. As we get more involved in the church, we may find that we spend all of our energy participating in events that focus on the church community – inwardly focused events – even though our whole mission statement is supposed to steer our vision upwards and outwards.

LOCKED IN THE CHURCH BUILDING

Often this locked-in culture spreads right down to the geography of our lives. For many of us, our schedules physically revolve around the church building and we find ourselves spending a huge amount of time within the safety of its four walls.

I remember witnessing a classic example of this a few years ago. One of my friends was a member of his church's Facebook group, and this church was looking to work out a strategy of growth for the next six or seven years. As part of this, the church was asking for members of the group to post suggestions and ideas on the Facebook page.

A lot of suggestions made were for exciting new events that the church could run – some of them sounded great. But my friend had suggested that perhaps what the church needed was to spend less time doing 'church events' at the church and more time outside of the church investing in the local community. He proposed that rather than run a parenting course in the church one term, the church could maybe encourage people to get down to the local pub and meet parents in the area. Then, over time, they could invite the same people to do a parenting course – maybe hosted in the pub.

Now, my friend doesn't run a church and he would be the first to admit that any suggestion he makes should be taken with a healthy pinch of salt, but to me this seemed like a really sensible suggestion. Something a bit different that the church could try! But despite this, he was shot down very quickly. A member of the congregation replied to his post within minutes to suggest that, rather than focusing the church's efforts on engaging with people outside of the church premises they should – you've guessed it – run a new evening event at the church. I wish I was joking!

The problem with basing all church life within the church building is that for someone who is not a part of church culture, it can feel completely alien. Many people will spend their whole lives having never set foot in a church building – you may have even heard people exclaim, 'Me? I'd burn if I stepped in a church!' For many people, a faith-based activity in a church building will make them feel like a fish out of water – and that's if they even pluck up the courage to swim through the front door.

I have been around churches my whole life; I am very comfortable with how they work and what Christian events entail. I
would also say I'm fairly confident and outgoing. Despite all of
that, I have sometimes felt so intensely uncomfortable in church,
especially if it's a new church or a church I am just visiting.
Standing alone, surrounded by people whose mandate is to
'love' – it can be the loneliest place in the world. I'm sure most
of us will have felt like that at some point in our lives. Now,
imagine that discomfort and multiply it by a hundred. That's how
alien a church event may feel to someone who hasn't been to
church before. For many Christians, the church is our safe space.
The problem is, if someone isn't a Christian, it probably isn't
theirs.

THE EXCLUSIVE CHURCH CULTURE

I am probably not alone in feeling that, more than just the church
buildings and calendar, this locked-in problem also spreads right
down to our Christian language and culture. Actually, the two are
linked because a major part of being a member of a certain culture
is being fluent in that culture's individual 'language'. In the church
we sometimes call it 'Christianese'. It's a language we're all uncon-
sciously fluent in. For instance, I was told a story by a trainee vicar
who was sitting next to a friend who was relatively new to church.
About halfway through the service, the speaker got up on the stage
and started his message: 'I want to speak about grace today. Grace
is so wonderful. You cannot beat the beauty of grace, however hard
you try.'

His unchurched friend leaned over to him and whispered, 'Who's
Grace?'

If you've spent much time around the church, then grace is a concept you'll be completely familiar with. Yet grace is not a word in common usage outside of the church, so people are often completely thrown off when we use words like that.

And it's not just grace. We have a whole go-to vocabulary reserved for the use of Christians. The effect of this language, and the effect of any exclusive language, is to create an 'us and them' mentality – those of us who are fluent in Christianese and those people who frankly find it weird. Having an exclusive language immediately sets up barriers between 'us' and those 'not like us'.

And Christianese culture is deeper than just the language we use; it extends to clothing, books (like this one, incidentally), media and music. There is a Christian version of almost everything – dig deep enough and you even have Christian diets! None of these things is problematic in and of itself; for instance, listening to Christian music is great – just think of how excited my twelve-year-old self was to see Delirious?! Yet these aspects of Christian culture often betray our inward focus, because they demonstrate very obviously that we are somehow disconnected from mainstream society.

We could argue that the church is meant to be disconnected from mainstream culture, but that's not completely true. The church is called to be a part of mainstream culture, but at the same time to be radically different within it. That is to say, we're called to be in the world but not of the world. I don't think there's anything wrong with speaking fluent Christianese (you'll note this book even uses Christianese phrases!), but we need to make sure it's not the only language we're comfortable using, otherwise we will never be able to connect with the community outside of our churches – the community that we as a church actually exist to reach.

HEALTHY, OUTWARD-LOOKING CHURCH

Now you may be sitting, reading this, raging in your chair. Why shouldn't the church look after its own? People in mainstream culture have largely rejected the Christian faith, so why should we pursue them?

Such a response is understandable. However you look at it, large portions of the church are being rejected by society. Whether that is reflected in falling church attendances and levels of Christian belief,[9] or court cases where Christian values are rejected in favour of secular values,[10] our culture is increasingly less 'Christian' in terms of its attitudes, beliefs and behaviours. And so it's easy for us to feel marginalized as Christians in our faith.

In this climate, it is only natural for us to seek shelter. It's only natural for us to want to find a comfort zone where we feel our values aren't being attacked and we can surround ourselves with people who have a similar outlook to us. But we know there's more to our faith than finding a comfort zone.

At its heart, this is not how Jesus wanted his followers to spend their time. Take Jesus' parable of the mustard seed, found in Matthew 13:31–32:

He told them another parable: 'The kingdom of heaven is like a mustard seed, which a man took and planted in his field. Though it is the smallest of all seeds, yet when it grows, it is the largest of garden plants and becomes a tree, so that the birds come and perch in its branches.'

At first, this parable seems to be all about the similarities between a mustard seed and God's kingdom. Have you ever seen mustard seeds in a pot of grainy mustard? They're tiny things, but despite this small size they can rapidly grow into a tree four metres high (though probably not if they've already been turned into mustard). And that's kind of like God's kingdom: it has a humble beginning in all of our lives, but it also has the capacity to grow and dominate who we are. That is a great and serious message in itself, but there is another level of meaning to this parable.

Jesus' audience would have been very familiar with the Old Testament – in an age without lots of books, they would have been much more familiar with it than we are today. And when Jesus talks about the kingdom of God being like a tree, he is using a picture first mentioned in Psalm 104, and then developed by both Ezekiel and Daniel in their books in the Old Testament. In Jesus' parable, he borrows the language and imagery used in these pictures to remind his audience of them.

The prophecies in Ezekiel, Daniel and Psalm 104 were given and developed at a time when Israel was at an all-time low and the idea behind them is that God will restore the glory of his kingdom Israel – and the image used to describe this restored kingdom is a tree.

Here's Ezekiel 17:22–23, and God is speaking:

> I myself will take a shoot from the very top of a cedar and
> plant it; I will break off a tender sprig from its topmost shoots
> and plant it on a high and lofty mountain. On the mountain
> heights of Israel I will plant it; it will produce branches and
> bear fruit and become a splendid cedar. Birds of every kind
> will nest in it; they will find shelter in the shade of its branches.

In the Middle East, the cedar was the biggest and most impressive
tree around. And in this passage, God suggests that his restored
kingdom will be like that cedar tree: impressive, strong and durable.
And in Jesus' picture he echoes this image of restoration. Notice
that both Ezekiel and Jesus say:

> Birds of every kind will nest in [the tree]; they will find
> shelter in the shade of its branches.

This metaphor is explained in Ezekiel 31, where he tells us that the
birds of the air refer to all the nations of the Earth. So as the
kingdom of God grows up into this beautiful tall tree, all the
nations around are attracted to it and find shelter in it. Jesus and
Ezekiel are making a very clear point here: God's kingdom exists
to serve the nations; by its very nature, God's kingdom has an
outward focus.

Jesus really hammered this point home. You'll notice that he talked
about a mustard tree while Ezekiel talked about a cedar. That
wasn't a mistake! Jesus hadn't misremembered the picture; he was

shocking his audience to tell them that God's kingdom would not be what they were expecting.

Many Jews at the time thought that Ezekiel's picture was all about prospering their country and their people. They thought that when God restored his kingdom, it would be all about Israel becoming great again. Actually, Jesus was telling them that it's not about that at all. He was shocking them into the realization that God's kingdom was all about the outsider, the poor and the down-trodden. It was intended to bless and serve the 'other'.

And that is as true today as it was 2,000 years ago. God does not want us simply to erect a billboard outside of the church for passers-by to stare at. He wants our very existence to be focused on serving and blessing those who are not yet part of the church.

I'm not saying that our church culture, activities or even bill-boards are bad things (especially if they are punny). I wouldn't discourage anyone from getting stuck in, and some of these activities are vital. The church needs to be cared for and invested in. The problem comes when we find ourselves spending our whole lives doing church-focused and church-based events, rather than spending time actually engaging with and serving our broader communities.

THE PROBLEM WITH BEING LOCKED IN

Being locked in poses a real threat to our collective health as a church. How can we hope to have an influence on culture if we are not actively engaging with it?

At school, when I was fourteen or fifteen, I was a bit of a geek. I would often do pretty well in my classes, but I wasn't considered particularly 'cool' or hip by my friends. I was kind of bombing at all of those things that made people popular at our school, like being in a relationship (I had never had a proper girlfriend, despite trying desperately hard), being good at sports or being tall and good-looking.

But then one girl astounded the entire year by taking an interest in me. I still can't believe that she did; she was way out of my league! But for some reason she decided to talk to me and eventually we started dating. We dated for about two months until she left the school. In that time, I changed so much. I changed my hairstyle and clothes, I started listening to popular bands, and during that time people started to see me in a different light. Suddenly I was a bit more popular.

None of those changes was forced on me. I don't think this girl asked me to change anything. I was just gradually transformed as I spent time with someone who was quite different from me. I almost absorbed or took on some of her identity without even meaning to. As I did, some of her popularity rubbed off on me.

Relationships change us. It is impossible to influence someone if we don't have a connection with them. People are transformed by other people; we develop and grow through relationships. That's the nature of being human.

That's important for us as we deal with the church's locked-in syndrome. We're going to struggle to have a transformative influence if we don't have relationships with people not already in church. And I'm not talking about token friendships or a symbolic presence, but about real and vulnerable relationships. Who is going to influence you more: the kind guy that smiles and waves at you when you pass him on the pavement every morning, or the best friend walking beside you every step of the way? We need to be best friends with people who aren't already in church, not just kind men and women smiling and waving at passers-by. They might well appreciate that gesture, but nine times out of ten, people will go to their best friend when they need help, not the kind but casual acquaintance.

The danger is that, as a church, we sometimes choose to suffer this locked-in syndrome because of fear. If we were to become more active outside of our church walls, it would be uncomfortable, it would get messy and people would probably get hurt along the way. Vulnerability is painful. It takes sweat and sacrifice. But you can't find those opportunities to transform the world from within your comfort zone. They only come from that place of vulnerability.

Jesus doesn't ask us to make a comfortable, safe community for ourselves. He asks us to go to the lost, the broken and the destitute – and he asks us to bring the good news to those people. Jesus wants us outside of our comfortable church walls, transforming the world in his name. If we truly want to follow him, then we need to walk with him as he goes to those people.

CONCLUSION

We have seen how the church is supposed to be an outwardly focused institution; we've looked at how it exists to make disciples of all nations and bring God's kingdom to Earth. However, we have also seen that despite being enthusiastic for that growth, our churches are often structured in a way that is inwardly focused, often due to our (completely natural) desire to be comfortable.

This leads to a locked-in culture and means that we struggle to provide a transformative edge in our society. Without real, vulnerable connections with people outside of the church, we struggle to exert a transformational influence.

So far, reading this book, you may be feeling that the illness of the church is pretty severe, maybe even terminal? Don't worry, it's not! The 'diagnosis' and, more importantly, the 'cure' are in sight. We just need to look at one further symptom before we begin to identify the underlying cause.

3 The symptoms
The Elephant Man

THE UNAPPEALING CHURCH

'Actually, I'm a Christian.' My statement rang out in the uncomfortable silence. I say uncomfortable silence; actually, I would describe it as the most uncomfortable silence of my life. No-one knew what to say; like with the cherished but slightly racist grandparent who starts making politically incorrect statements about immigration at dinner, nobody really knew how to respond.

It was the first day of university and I had just met a group of medical students. We had all gone for lunch at a hipster sandwich shop down the road from our campus in South Kensington in London. Just as we had been sitting down, one of the girls came out with the most incredible question: 'So, what's everybody's favourite sex position?' Now, I wouldn't have said I was overly sheltered when I arrived at university, but I was quite sure that back in my home town that wouldn't have passed as polite lunchtime conversation. I mean, I was trying to eat a sandwich!

But, it being freshers' week, nobody wanted to seem naïve or prudish, so one by one everyone in the group answered the question. Some of the things people came out with, I was pretty certain they were making it up. First, there was 'the pile driver' – now, I'm fairly sure that's actually a wrestling move. Then there were the boys who each named their favourite positions after increasingly exotic animals – I'm pretty sure they were all virgins. But nobody wanted to seem out of touch or naïve, so the whole room just nodded along in agreement: 'Yeah, I'm a big fan of the Tyrannosaurus Rex too!'

And we went on like that until it came to me. At this point I realized I had a choice to make. I could also invent an outlandish sex position or I could come clean about both my virginity and my Christianity. And for me, at the time, there was no choice to make. I told them that I didn't agree with sex before marriage, and then followed it up with the haymaker: 'I'm a Christian.'

Three little words that can completely change the course of a conversation! Sadly though, that change in course is increasingly to stormier waters. These days, I find that confessing my faith rarely ends well in polite conversation.

It's not that I'm ashamed of my faith. It's not that I dislike talking about it either, but I do dislike confrontation. Upsetting people really doesn't sit well with me, especially if I can avoid it. And, over the last seven or eight years, I've found that nothing upsets people more than declaring that I'm a Christian.

It's like we're modern-day elephant men. The Elephant Man was a Victorian gentleman called Joseph Merrick who began developing disfiguring deformities within a few years of being born. These deformities worsened until he became a social outcast. He was eventually disowned by his family and sent to the workhouse. After a period there – seemingly as a way out of poverty – he allowed himself to be exhibited, like a circus attraction, to horrified Victorian crowds. They came to stare at him because they had never seen someone so disfigured. The world of medicine still doesn't know what caused these deformities; several conditions have been suggested but nothing has been proven conclusively.

The Elephant Man spent his life as an outcast; when he wasn't socially isolated he was being exhibited like an animal in a zoo. Sometimes, when I am sitting with people who aren't Christians, if I start talking about my faith it feels as though, rather than seeing me, all they can make out is some modern-day Elephant Man babbling nonsense. They stare at me with horrified expressions, as if they've never heard of something so disfiguring. I pray that you have never experienced such a response, but I fear that you may understand more than a little of what I'm talking about.

IT IS THE SICK THAT NEED A DOCTOR

In my first year practising as a doctor, I worked in a ward where we cared for a lot of patients with liver ailments. One of the most common problems people have with their livers is alcohol-related damage. There was one particular patient whom I will never forget.

He was an alcoholic and he would come in with a big, fat tummy full of liquid. It looked like he was heavily pregnant, except rather than having a baby in his abdomen, he had litres and litres of straw-coloured fluid inside him. It's a common symptom with liver disease and it often indicates a severely damaged liver. When he came in he would always be in a real state: his tummy was so full he would be unable to walk. He was living with another alcoholic who would buy him alcohol and leave him on the sofa. He would sit at home drinking and drinking until he became unconscious. Walking was such a challenge to him that, at times, he wouldn't be able to get up to use the bathroom; he'd just soil himself on the sofa.

He would come into hospital in this awful state, but after a few days of medical care he would be just well enough to walk to the front of the hospital and get in a taxi to go home. And he did. We couldn't stop him. He had the capacity to make decisions about his own health and we have to respect a patient's wishes. This particular patient would come in, receive just enough care to become well enough to leave, then self-discharge from the hospital.

As a doctor, I cannot treat people who do not wish to be treated. In a similar way, the church cannot help people who won't let us near them. In Jesus' time the Pharisees were those people. They thought they had it all together, they thought they knew the way to heaven and so they resisted Jesus' teaching and his authority. Instead they relied on strict rules and regulations to work their way to the kingdom of God.

Today, much of society has given up on God's kingdom and, instead, we set about busily building our own. We fill the gaping void in our lives with wealth, possessions and relationships. The problem is, no matter how large or beautiful or well curated our kingdoms are, they are still hollow and empty imitations of the true kingdom that we were all intended to inhabit. Remember what Tozer said in his book *The Pursuit of God*? The human heart is made to pursue God, but so often we look to other worldly things to fill the 'God-shaped hole' in our lives. The church is supposed to point the way to Jesus and his kingdom; it is in Jesus that people find true satisfaction. But when the church suggests our culture may not have all the answers, we are greeted like the Elephant Man. People are repulsed by us and our gospel is mocked as out of touch. Not by everyone, and not all the time – but I'm sure the majority of us could share examples of this.

For me – and I imagine for you also – being seen as an Elephant Man is a major problem. If we want to turn around the situation of the church and truly transform our culture, we're always going to struggle to have this transformative influence within a society that finds us physically repulsive.

Now, there have always been those who hear gospel truth and respond, and those who find it repulsive – like large parts of the religious establishment in the gospels. So this begs the question: is our society's repulsion at the church and Christians in general just a normal response that a proportion of people will always have when confronted with the Truth? Or, just maybe, does our modern-day society present other sorts of obstacles to sharing the gospel?

WHAT SINS?

Western culture is one of the most liberal on Earth. We place an incredibly high value on freedom. We can also be incredibly individualistic. Our emphasis on freedom combined with this individualistic attitude means that the thing that we value above all else is the freedom of the individual – the individual person must be free to do what they want to do. Furthermore, Western society can be very hedonistic: we place a very high value (perhaps not consciously) on pleasing ourselves and doing the things that bring us enjoyment. These three characteristics of liberalism (being free), individualism (being first) and hedonism (prioritizing things that please us) create a mantra common in our society, especially among people under thirty-five, which can be summed up as: 'The most important thing is that I am free to do the things that please me.'

So if you tell someone who holds this attitude that Jesus loves them and died for their sins, they'd likely respond, 'What sins?' In a world that considers that doing the things which please oneself is the most important thing, there are very few things that are considered 'sins'. With this attitude, as long as we don't commit crimes like murder or rape, we can consider ourselves 'good people'.

As I mentioned at the start of this book, I grew up in a seaside town called Weston-Super-Mare, and a lot of my friends and family still live there. I love hearing the stories of transformation and change that they tell me about Weston. It is unique among the towns of the UK in that it hosts 11% of the UK's drug and alcohol rehabilitation centres.[11] For a town of roughly 80,000 people, that is a huge amount! Within the last few years, St Paul's Weston (the church that my family and many friends attend) has developed a very healthy ministry among this population of recovering addicts. There has been an amazing response to the gospel within this group and they now have some of the most amazing stories of transformation to share.

I think that part of the reason for this amazing response to the gospel is the situation in which these addicted people find themselves. When you've admitted that you're an addict, you really know that you're a broken person. For many of us, it can be easy to pretend that we're not broken. But when you've lost everything because of your addiction, when you're destitute and homeless because of your habit, it's a lot easier to see that something isn't right. It's slightly more obvious to see that you need to be mended.

As a church, one of the major challenges facing us today is that people simply don't see the need to 'be mended'. We live such healthy, wealthy lives, relative to the rest of the world, that people struggle to see a need for God. What sin would we need Jesus to save us from? We're 'good people', after all.

I spent six years at university living with people who weren't Christians. One of them, another medical student, once met a group of Christians in our student bar. They got talking and he realized that they knew me. He went on to have a long conversation with them, explaining how he could see the importance that my faith held for me. He said that he could always tell when I'd been in church because there was such a difference in me when I came home afterwards. When I heard of this conversation, it stirred mixed emotions in me. On the one hand, I was overjoyed at the way that he could see the impact my faith was having in my life. But on the other hand I was really upset that, despite seeing the amazing change that my faith causes in me, he didn't want to buy into that himself. And this is the thing: he doesn't see a need for that impact in his own life because he doesn't consider himself broken and in need of repair. He is an amazing man – by any standard of the world he is a 'good person', indeed one of the best – but by God's standards all have sinned and fallen short. But the vast majority of other people in our nation don't see it like that.

There is the old saying 'familiarity breeds contempt', and in the case of the gospel I think that it's true. Many people assume that they already know what the gospel is about and have already decided that it isn't for them.

I remember once doing a talk on evangelism. After the talk, I spoke to a girl who wanted some help in her attempts to evangelize. She explained that her friends at school didn't want to listen when she talked about her faith because they said they already knew what she was talking about. According to them, they were gospel experts. She asked them what they thought it was all about, and of course none of them really had any idea. They could recite some Christian clichés and gospel truisms that had been forced down their throat during school assemblies, but they didn't have any grasp of what the gospel truly meant.

The problem this girl faced was, because they had grown up in a 'Christian country' and attended a church school, they thought their understanding of Christianity was pretty spot on – so they didn't want to hear any more about it.

It's a bit like 'poverty fatigue'. This is the idea that over the years there have been so many charity adverts on television showing graphic images of poverty and brokenness that they now fail to shock us. Whereas once these campaigns were very profitable for charities, as their sad images pulled on viewers' heartstrings (and purse strings), we have now reached the point where few bother to respond because – due to the sheer volume – they are desensitized to these terrible images.

I wonder if we have a similar phenomenon of 'gospel fatigue' in our society? Having grown up around churches and Christianity, people are so familiar with the gospel, or at least think they are, that gospel mantras such as 'all have sinned and fallen short of God's glory' and 'Jesus loves you' have ceased to have any real meaning. People think that they've heard it all before and don't want to hear it all again.

PR DIFFICULTIES

The problem isn't just that people don't realize they're broken or have gospel fatigue. It's also that, even if people did realize they needed help, they probably wouldn't go to the church to get mended!

Our society is incredibly sexualized: our advertising, our film industry and our magazines are full of sexual imagery. A 2007 study found that the average single man watches forty minutes of pornographic material three times a week, while men in relationships 'only' watched twenty minutes of material 1.7 times a week. Terrifyingly, this study failed to find any men who did not use pornography – sex is everywhere[12] and consequently sexual freedom is the paramount value of our culture. Above all else, people in our culture want to be free to express their sexuality as they wish.

Within this context, as a church we have taken a fairly contrary view to that of much of society. You probably don't need me to remind you that this has resulted in some fairly poor PR for the church!

At the same time, our society has grown increasingly distrustful of large institutions. As a generation, so many of us feel let down by those institutions that make up the fabric of our country. From bankers and politicians to businesses and police federations, none of the large institutions of our country has managed to escape the growing distrust and dissatisfaction that we feel – and tragically, that includes the church.

These days, and particularly within younger generations, 'big' organizations are viewed with suspicion. Generally, they are seen to be self-serving, sometimes 'corrupt' and generally more focused on protecting their interests than looking after 'ordinary' people like us.

This causes real difficulty for us as a church seeking to share our faith: if people have questions like 'Why am I here?' or 'What is the purpose in life?', given this general climate and the poor PR we have faced as a church, are they going to come knocking on our door? Or are they going to treat our answers with suspicion and distrust? Sadly, it seems that people often take the latter option.

JOHN'S REJECTION

In John 15:19, Jesus says, 'If you were of the world, the world would love its own; but because you are not of the world, but I chose you out of the world, because of this the world hates you' (NASB).

On the surface, this verse may very easily apply to us. Jesus is teaching that his audience are hated because they were so unlike the world that they were inhabiting. Sounds a lot like us, yes? But I'm not sure it's that simple.

It is likely that John's Gospel was written to a community of Jews who had accepted Jesus as their Saviour. After accepting Jesus, this particular group continued to associate with other Jews, who hadn't accepted Jesus as Messiah, with the hope that they could change people's minds. Unsurprisingly, their continued involvement in the Jewish community led to increasing tensions until it seems they were expelled from the community and the synagogue.

That expulsion created a lot of hurt in John's community, and so when he writes his gospel to them and uses teaching like the above, he is specifically addressing their personal rejection by the Jewish community. And those Jews rejected John's group precisely because they were a continuing presence in the Jewish community but they were not like that Jewish community; they believed the Messiah had arrived (something the other Jews were still waiting for), they lived differently and, in the eyes of those Jews, they worshipped a different God.

But are we really 'in the world' in the same way? For some of us, the answer is arguably no. We might pass through 'the world', but the time we spend actually 'living' – the time that we can choose to spend how we please, the time in which we are open and vulnerable – is spent in the church. For others, I think we may resemble the world more than we would like to admit.

Yes, some of us might disagree with sex before marriage, and others may hold differing views on the topics of euthanasia or abortion; we may try not to drink too much and we might say no to drugs; but many of us still buy into the culture of this world. We throw ourselves headlong into the cult of celebrity, we still worry about pleasing the idol of 'self', we define ourselves by our relationship status, we are seduced by mass media and marketing into chasing after a dream of wealth and freedom in the hope that it will fill the hole in our lives.

Although we may be serious about our faith, culturally many of us do engage with a lot of similar behaviours to our 'world'. So, unlike John's community, we are not rejected by our culture because we are in the world but so unlike it. Instead, we are rejected because we are often isolated from it and yet, in some ways, too similar to it.

The world has looked at the church, preaching these high-minded moral values, but has seen a movement of people who sometimes look pretty similar to them: people who have not been radically changed by those values. The world has seen a movement of people who talk about the greatest, most selfless gift humanity has ever been given, but who still often buy into the consumeristic, individualistic, materialistic values of our culture.

And society says to themselves, if these people have such an amazing thing going on, why are they not more affected by it? Many of us will have heard the statement 'You are the only Bible that some people will ever read', but if we are not being personally transformed by the Bible, perhaps we more closely resemble an issue of *Glamour* magazine!

THE CHURCH IS A BASTION OF GOD'S KINGDOM

'In the world but not of the world' is a phrase many of us will have heard before. Actually, it's a hallmark phrase of Christianese! To 'unpack' this phrase further (another commonly used word in the church!), the church is meant to be an outpost of God's perfect kingdom surrounded by, and interacting with, a broken world. Jesus calls us to be in the world in a real and vulnerable way. We are called to weep with those who weep, rejoice with those who rejoice, bind up the broken and serve the poor. At the same time, we are called to be radically different from the world, to reject the consumeristic, materialistic, sexualized culture that we inhabit. We are called to serve Jesus and seek his kingdom first. The church is supposed to reflect God in such a way that to experience the church is to grasp something of God's kingdom already present on Earth.

CONCLUSION

At the start of this chapter, we looked at whether being allocated our Elephant Man status is the natural reaction people will always have to the gospel. We looked at how our particular generation presents a unique situation: in today's culture the concept of sin or needing a saviour is alien and so many do not see a need for the gospel. We have suffered particularly bad PR in the past few decades and finally, as a church culture, we can find ourselves socially isolated from the world but not necessarily distinct culturally, leading to confusion for those outside the church.

Add this to the previous two chapters – some delirious disciples and, in places, a severe case of locked-in syndrome – and it sounds like we might have a sick patient on our hands. Yet it is only when we analyse the symptoms and diagnose the underlying problem that we can prescribe a treatment and truly start to get better again.

What I want to do now in the 'diagnosis' is to consider the underlying problem causing all these symptoms in a little more depth. If we want to transform our culture and turn around the situation of the church – if we want ourselves individually and the church collectively to be as healthy as Jesus empowers us to be – we need to get this bit right.

The diagnosis

- ☐ God's Kingdom and the gospel
- ☐ The Selfish Gospel
- ☐ The Selfish Gospel at work

4 The diagnosis
God's kingdom and the gospel

HIS GOSPEL IS NOT OUR GOSPEL

As we began our journey of diagnosis, I suggested that the problems we have identified are not isolated issues, but all symptoms of one underlying problem. Just as a cough, runny nose and sore throat are not separate diseases but symptoms of one underlying cold, I think we can trace the root cause of our three issues back to one root problem. Our gospel often minimizes the kingdom of God. Why? Because our gospel is often selfish – *gulp*. Let me explain.

At the age of ten, I committed my life to Jesus and began a relationship with him. But, in the eyes of my ten-year-old self, there was a problem: I hadn't experienced the Holy Spirit. Or at least, I wasn't sure if I had! I had grown up in a Charismatic part of the church, and in my head I associated relationship with Jesus with very clear physical manifestations in the Holy Spirit – whether that be tingling hands, shaky legs or an overwhelming desire to cry uncontrollably. I worried that because I had never experienced a clear and physical 'baptism in the Spirit', I wasn't a real Christian.

This really concerned me. I thought I had done something wrong; I thought perhaps I was a faulty Christian. My deepest fear was that somehow when I'd said my 'sinner's prayer' and given my life to God, he had somehow missed it. Perhaps God's attention had been elsewhere or he had just misheard me. And perhaps subsequently, the Holy Spirit had missed me out when he was doing the rounds.

This fear persisted on and off for a good three years, and for a while it seemed like I was stuck on repeat: because I worried that I wasn't a 'real' Christian, every time there was an invitation during a church meeting to come to the front as a symbolic action that I wanted to invite Jesus into my heart, I would go forward.

I'd always pray, 'God, we both know that I've been here several times before, but I'm still not convinced you've heard me, and I really don't want to miss out on this, so just in case you missed it, or I didn't say it right, I'm going to stand here and say this all again.' I did it over and over; I think my parents actually worried about me.

But every time I stood up there and started to pray this prayer, my words were always fairly similar. First I would thank God for loving and creating me; next I would thank him for Jesus and his death on the cross. Then I would confess my own sin and brokenness, and finally I would ask him to forgive me and accept me into relationship with him. Everyone would clap and I'd often be given a Bible – I managed to gather quite a collection.

And that's all great, but notice the sinner's prayer that I was led through each time: it would always focus on the themes of creation by a loving God, the fall of mankind and my personal sin, redemption through Jesus' death and resurrection, and then the beginning of a new relationship with Jesus, often with me 'asking Jesus into my heart'. I was taught that by saying this prayer, I would avoid eternal damnation and receive the gift of eternal life. This is all wonderfully and brilliantly true.

But compare this message to the one that Jesus preached. His message, although it touched on all of the above, was more focused on the arrival of God's kingdom. Look at these verses from the gospels:

> After John was put in prison, Jesus went into Galilee, proclaiming the good news of God. 'The time has come,' he said. '**The kingdom of God has come near**. Repent and believe the good news!' (Mark 1:14–15)

> Jesus went throughout Galilee, teaching in their synagogues, proclaiming the **good news of the kingdom**, and healing every disease and illness among the people. (Matthew 4:23)

> [Jesus] said to them, 'I must preach **the kingdom of God** to the other cities also, for I was sent for this purpose.' (Luke 4:43, NASB)

> ... **this gospel of the kingdom** will be preached in the whole world as a testimony to all nations ... (Matthew 24:14)

Do you notice how each of these passages focuses more on the kingdom of God than the theme of forgiveness of sins? How they all indicate that the kingdom of God is the central theme of the gospel? If we step back from individual verses and start to look at the entire body of Jesus' recorded teaching, what we see is that the kingdom of God was the major focus of what he said.

In his book *Surprised by Hope: Rethinking Heaven, the Resurrection and the Mission of the Church*, Tom Wright agrees, noting that most Christians 'remain satisfied with what is at best a truncated and distorted view of the great biblical hope'.[13]

Ronald Sider goes further. In his 2005 book, *The Scandal of the Evangelical Conscience*, he said:

> One of the most astonishing ironies of contemporary Evangelicalism is that most Evangelicals do not even define the gospel the way that Jesus did! . . . Jesus did not define the gospel as the forgiveness of sins, although again and again he offered free, unmerited forgiveness. The vast majority of New Testament scholars today, whether evangelical or liberal, agree that the central aspect of Jesus' teaching was the gospel of the Kingdom of God. Forgiveness of sins is at the centre of Jesus' proclamation of the gospel of the kingdom. But it is only part of it.[14]

Jesus did not simply preach about the forgiveness of sins. He preached the necessity of repentance and the forgiveness of sins in the light of the fact that God's kingdom had arrived. The arrival of God's kingdom was the major news of the gospel, and repentance is a necessary consequence of that.

Jesus taught that God's glorious will was going to be accomplished on Earth, both through the person of Jesus and to be continued by Jesus' followers when he left. What was that will? It was the restoration of the Earth and the return of righteousness, peace and justice; that is the kingdom of God, that is his manifest will, and that is the gospel! It is the work Jesus began, the work he will finish, but also the work we are invited to be a part of in the meantime.

However, when we pray a sinner's prayer, we rarely mention God's kingdom – it often doesn't get a look in. At best, we hint at themes of God's kingdom by discussing Jesus' sacrificial death on the cross. Of course, this is the heart of the kingdom – the gospel must never be less than this – but just as there is more to a body than a heart, there is more to God's kingdom than Jesus' death on the cross.

It's like this: Jesus did not just die on the cross, swan off back to heaven and leave us to wait it out until we die and go to heaven to be with him. And yet, sadly, that's often the impression our gospel gives. Jesus came to Earth to proclaim the arrival of God's kingdom. By that, he was preaching that all of creation was going to be restored. A central part of that restoration was Jesus' death on the cross, but that isn't the end of the story. Thank God (literally!).

We were each saved for a purpose. We weren't saved by Jesus so that we could float around in a Christian bubble eating quiche and drinking weak orange squash until we die and go to heaven. We were saved by Jesus for the purpose of continuing the work that he started.

But when we preach the gospel, we manage to uncouple the idea of forgiveness of sins from the kingdom of God. We rarely say, 'Repent and enter the kingdom of God' when sharing the gospel, perhaps because we feel it is too difficult a concept to communicate to new Christians. Instead, we simply say, 'Repent because Jesus loves you.'

The effect that this has is to make it seem like the tale ends there. The gospel is the greatest story ever told, but it didn't end when Jesus died on the cross; it ends when Jesus returns to fully bring in his kingdom and restore the fullness of creation in all its entirety. In the meantime, we are called to faithfully bring God's kingdom to Earth, empowered by the Holy Spirit. This isn't some optional extra, it's a key part of the gospel message. It's all part of the same story.

Pete Hughes, the leader of vibrant London church KXC, explains this concept in his forthcoming book *All Things New* in three words: Creation – Decreation – Recreation. Creation is the beginning in Genesis, where we are in a state of perfect relationship with God. Decreation is the fall of humanity, where Adam and Eve ate the forbidden fruit and were cast out of the Garden of Eden. It's a story we are all part of because we've all fallen short of God's perfect standards. Pete explains that we find ourselves somewhere in the space between Decreation and Recreation. Recreation is the goal we are journeying towards in our Christian faith. The story isn't over yet; we haven't reached the destination. The story starts just as we invite Jesus into our lives.

To steal some imagery from the Bible, the church of Christ is the hope of the nations, a city built on a hill, a light shining in the darkness. We are God's agent for change on Earth. If we preach the forgiveness of sins without preaching the arrival of God's kingdom, we are stopping the story halfway through.

WHY THE KINGDOM OF GOD?

I think a big part of the problem is that God's kingdom is very misunderstood. The phrase 'the kingdom of God' is one that many Christians use, but very few truly grasp.

God's kingdom is not some shining city made of gold, floating in clouds; it does not simply mean 'heaven', as many of us may think. God's kingdom is not a physical place at all. Instead, it is best understood as meaning God's rule and reign. When the kingdom of God is present, God's perfect will is unfolding in that place. That situation is restored and reconciled with God's plans and purposes.

The vast majority of Jesus' recorded teaching in the gospels relates to the kingdom of God. For instance, in the Sermon on the Mount, Jesus isn't just talking about how we should behave as 'good Christians'. He is talking about the ethical and moral aspects of the new kingdom that he is bringing into being. This is a kingdom characterized by God's deep love, with a stated aim of transforming the world so that it is restored to its pre-fall, pre-sin state. Justice, peace and righteousness are the hallmarks of this kingdom.

God's kingdom advances every time we choose to follow Jesus and sacrificially love someone; it grows whenever an aspect of creation, however small, is restored in line with God's perfect will. The kingdom of God is a revolution of sacrificial love. The church's mission is to bring that kingdom of God into being as best we can, until Jesus returns to complete that mission.

I think that to better grasp the revolutionary nature of God's kingdom, we have to understand it in the context of Jesus' ministry. To tell the gospel story without the kingdom of God is to take out one of the major plot points. It's like reading a book with every other page removed – the story doesn't really make sense. To really understand what I mean, we need to hear the gospel story through the lens of the kingdom of God.

To give us a fresh perspective, let's picture it as a film. This is in no way theologically accurate, but it helps us to grasp what's going on. Imagine it's 1970 and we're in New York, in the company of New York's most notorious gangs (I did tell you it wasn't theologically accurate!). In our film, the kingdom of God is like a hotly contested piece of territory and the various groups who oppose Jesus are represented by the gangs fighting over that territory.

First, you have the Pharisees; they were religious purists dedicated to preserving and obeying the Old Testament law. They were the ascendant group at the time of Jesus' ministry, kind of like an ambitious and powerful branch of the Italian Mafia in our film.

Next you have the Scribes, the teachers of the law. They acted as lawyers who copied the Old Testament law (hence the term scribe), but also as religious teachers who worked out detailed rules based on interpretations of the law, in order to apply it to everyday situations. They were like the lawyers and bankers who take the Mafia's money and enable them to continue their empire of crime.

The third group are the Sadducees; they were the other main politico-religious group at the time of Jesus. The Sadducees were predominantly wealthy landowners, most chief priests were also Sadducees and they were the dominant party of the Sanhedrin (Jewish supreme council). They were much more conservative than the Pharisees and only believed in the first five books of the Old Testament. However, their power was fading by the time Jesus was teaching. For the purposes of our film, think of them as an ageing branch of the Mafia. These guys used to run the city, but now their networks of power are crumbling and they are clinging to what they can.

Then you have the Herodians, thought to be a political group that supported King Herod at the time. Think of these guys as the corrupt politicians who tolerate the Mafia as a means to power.

Finally, you have the Romans. They were the occupying force in Palestine, where Jesus was teaching. Their power rested in their military might and they used it to enforce the rule of law. For the most part they let the Jewish people get on with their religious practices, unless they were causing problems or inciting violence. In our film these guys are like the police; they hold all the power and they know it. They will take down any of the groups without distinction, but some of them were probably corrupt and under the influence of the gangs.

In every gangster film there's always a hero that rubs the gangs up the wrong way. In our film this is Jesus. Typically, the separate gangs put aside their differences to unite against the hero in order to defeat him. The same thing happens with Jesus. Despite many of their apparent differences, in the gospels we see the groups unite in opposition of Jesus. Beating him appeared the lesser of two evils.

THE ARRIVAL OF THE KINGDOM

So, in the gospels the kingdom of God is like a piece of contested territory. Different gangs have different ideas about what sort of place it will be. More than that, they all hold wildly differing views on how it will come in and what it will mean. One of the most popular theories about the kingdom of God at the time of Jesus was promoted by the Pharisees and Scribes. They were focused on outward observance of the Old Testament law, and the rules and traditions that they had built up from interpreting that law. It was their understanding that if they could encourage all Israel to keep those laws, rules and traditions, then God would bring in his kingdom. Then Israel would be great again! They saw the kingdom as bringing independence from Roman rule and ushering in a golden era for the Jewish people.

So the religious authorities, and especially the Pharisees, were focused on bringing the kingdom of God in through man's efforts. This serves as the gang's master plan in our film: their under-standing was that the kingdom would bring power, wealth and independence for Israel, and probably themselves personally, because as the religious leaders they would be given responsibility over this power and wealth. Other groups had differing ideas about the kingdom of God – or to put it another way, other gangs had alternative claims to this piece of territory – but on the whole, the Pharisees were the dominant players in the game.

But our fearless hero doesn't like this dastardly master plan! Jesus didn't like the Pharisees being in charge of this contested piece of territory. He actually taught something quite different from the Pharisees about the kingdom of God. This difference of opinion lay at the heart of the disagreement that led to his crucifixion – Jesus was interfering with what the Pharisees believed was the master plan.

And this disagreement centred on how the kingdom of God would be brought in. The Pharisees believed that the law directed people towards rule keeping and strict religiosity. But Jesus taught that the Old Testament law should actually point the people towards repentance. Hence in Mark 1:15 he proclaimed, 'The kingdom of God has come near. Repent and believe the good news.' While the Pharisees thought it was all about man's efforts to keep the law, Jesus taught that it was about man's attitude towards that law (which should be one of repentance), and in fact the kingdom of God was being brought in regardless of man's ability to comply.

In church circles we often talk about how the word 'gospel' means 'good news' – and many of us think that the good news is that God has forgiven our sins and wants to have a relationship with us. While that is good news (very good news indeed!) for us, that wouldn't have made sense for first-century Jews. They were God's chosen people; they already had a relationship with him. And they already had rituals for the forgiveness of their sins (such as the sacrificing of animals), as laid down in the Old Testament law. When Jesus preached good news to the Jews, the good news was that the kingdom of God was arriving at that time and in that place – something they were all waiting for – and even better, it was being brought in regardless of how well they kept the Old Testament law. That is the good news of the gospel.

So the Pharisees had this piece of kingdom of God territory stitched up; they were the gang in control and their master plan was slowly unfolding. And then in comes Jesus telling them they're wrong.

Initially they could ignore Jesus. Just as in every gangster film, the gangs tell themselves that he's a lone troublemaker and he'll soon go away. But Jesus doesn't go away: he makes a name for himself. People start to listen to him. He begins to tread on the toes of the various groups, preventing their master plan from proceeding and generally stopping them from accomplishing what they had set out to do. And Jesus was successful. People were listening to him and his teaching on the kingdom of God. And that meant they weren't paying as much attention to the Pharisees – or any other religious groups. Their powerbase was slipping away.

What's more, Jesus' teaching directly contradicted theirs. Whereas they shunned the sinners and the outcasts for failing to keep God's laws, Jesus actively sought those people out. He even suggested that they would be first in this new kingdom! Not only was Jesus contradicting the teaching of the Pharisees, he was actively attacking the rules and traditions the Pharisees lived by. He was pushing their master plan aside entirely.

So our gangs decide to hit back. They send people to challenge Jesus, to make a fool out of him or generally trick him into saying something that's wrong or stupid. But just as in every great gangster film, our hero can't be beaten. He defeats all these challengers and puts down their sneaky tricks and attacks.

In Mark 4:1–34, Jesus is preaching a series of parables about the kingdom of God. These parables are being preached directly after a series of conflicts with these different gangs, including the Pharisees (Mark 3:20–35), and this teaching should be seen as a direct response to that conflict. The suggestion throughout the whole passage of teaching is that the kingdom of God is not what the people were anticipating; the Pharisees and their master plan were wrong. Jesus directly contradicts the Pharisees' understanding of God's kingdom by telling his audience that God's kingdom has little to do with the effort of humanity and does not conform to man's expectations. Here's Mark 4:26–29:

> He also said, 'This is what the kingdom of God is like. A man scatters seed on the ground. Night and day, whether he sleeps or gets up, the seed sprouts and grows, though he does not know how. All by itself the soil produces corn – first the stalk, then the ear, then the full grain in the ear. As soon as the corn is ripe, he puts the sickle to it, because the harvest has come.'

The message of this parable is that God's kingdom confounds human reasoning and is not reliant on human action. The seeds represent God's kingdom, and they sprout no matter what man does. Man scatters the seeds and is used to reap the harvest, but aside from that he is completely surplus to requirements – he can't even understand how the seeds are growing! The flourishing of the seeds – or God's kingdom – is not reliant on man. Jesus is telling his audience that despite what the Pharisees have been teaching, it's not about mankind's efforts. The kingdom of God is not going to come in because of human obedience to the law. Instead Jesus said the kingdom of God was already arriving in his person.

Perhaps unsurprisingly, the Pharisees didn't take kindly to Jesus striking out their master plan. They didn't agree with his new teaching on the kingdom of God, and neither did most of the other religious factions. This tension between Jesus and these gangs builds throughout the gospels – they keep coming into conflict with Jesus and being defeated. As he becomes more popular, they become more and more disgruntled until eventually they put aside their differences and unite to stop him.

THE PINNACLE OF THE KINGDOM

United in their will to stop Jesus and his teaching, the various religious factions (the gangs in our film) are presented with the perfect opportunity to do this at the end of the gospels when Jesus comes to Jerusalem at Passover. This is the equivalent of Jesus leading a direct assault on the headquarters of our various gangs. Jerusalem was their powerbase and at Passover, Jews from all over the country would be visiting. Of course, all of these Jews would want to listen to this new teacher with his exciting proclamations about the kingdom of God. But that would mean they wouldn't be listening to the other religious groups, and so our gangs see Jesus' arrival in Jerusalem as a direct challenge to their power and authority.

They club together to stop him, regardless of the cost to themselves. They buy off one of Jesus' followers in an attempt to get close to him. They manage to seize Jesus in the dead of night and take him to the police (the Romans). They try to coerce the police into crucifying Jesus – that would put a stop to his meddling ways once and for all! But the Romans don't see what all the fuss is about; as far as they can tell, he hasn't done anything wrong. Eventually they are corrupted into following the will of the gangs, after some heavy persuasion, and they agree to crucify Jesus.

Like every good film climax, there is a profound twist. I can't imagine that the religious authorities had thought that Jesus' death would end in his resurrection and spawn a movement that has lasted for 2,000 years! They thought his death was the ultimate victory and the end of Jesus' ministry. But of course, this was really just the beginning because the cross was the ultimate victory for Jesus.

To understand this fully, we have to see the cross in the context of the kingdom of God. The cross was not only the climax of Jesus' ministry; it is also the pinnacle of the kingdom of God. Through Jesus' sacrificial death our sin was paid for, we take on Jesus' righteousness and, because of that, we are free to be in right relationship with God. In an ironic twist, Jesus' death at the hand of the religious authorities proved once and for all that the kingdom of God isn't about effort or application but about repentance and (the aspect we too often overlook) restoration.

The gangs thought they had won. But within forty days of Jesus' death, his followers are proclaiming his resurrection and continuing where Jesus left off, taking his new teaching on the kingdom of God to the ends of the known world. And the best bit? Jesus left the ending open to a sequel! He promises to return one day and bring in his kingdom in all his glory. And, as we anticipate his latest release, the blockbuster to end all blockbusters, Jesus asks each of us to build his kingdom. To make disciples of all people and work for his glory here on Earth.

Now, in describing the gospel narrative as a film about gangs in New York, I have vandalized the history of first-century Palestine and done the respective 'gangs' a great disservice. They weren't criminals and actually most of the groups were widely respected. Not for the first time in this book, I ask you please to forgive me!

A popular understanding of the Pharisees today is that they were self-serving hypocrites, focused only on their own power and wealth. By that understanding, perhaps they really were like a gang in 1970s New York. But although Jesus' teaching in the gospels suggests that this may have been true for some of them, at the time the Pharisees were seen as model Jews. They were respected and honoured and, as easy as it is to paint them as the bad guys, they certainly weren't seen like that at the time. Many of them were trying to get people to take an active interest in their faith, however misplaced their attempts may have been.

Regardless of that fact, to preach the gospel and leave out the kingdom of God doesn't make sense. Jesus' whole gospel was about the arrival of God's kingdom. The disagreements he had with the religious authorities centred on the kingdom of God. Jesus' crucifixion is the pinnacle of the kingdom and his final instructions are for us to make disciples of that kingdom – for us to continue building it. And of course, Jesus promises to come back and bring the kingdom in fully at the right time.

To tell the gospel without mentioning the kingdom of God leaves us focusing on themes such as forgiveness of sins and relationship with Jesus. While these themes are vitally important to the Christian message, they miss out a major part of what Jesus was seeking to establish – and what he will establish on his return.

CONCLUSION

We have seen that Jesus focused on the kingdom of God, but that it was poorly understood by his contemporary audience, just as it so often is today. In Jesus' time, the concept of the kingdom was wildly misunderstood by the religious authorities. Jesus' contrary teachings on the kingdom of God proved a major part of the disagreement that drives the gospel story and led to his death.

Today, our own understanding can lead us to tell only half of the gospel story; we preach repentance and forgiveness, but often neglect to mention God's kingdom and the call on us to step into it. This means we are only preaching half the story.

5 The diagnosis
The Selfish Gospel

THERE'S MORE TO THE STORY?

Without the kingdom of God we are sharing half the story – a story that doesn't make sense.

A few years ago my housemate Mike, a fellow medical student, was in hospital. He encountered a lady who was crippled with disease and was being intensively cared for. Because of her disease, she was severely disabled and without this help was quite incapable of looking after herself. Mike informed me that this lady was a Christian and spent almost all of her time listening to worship music and reading her Bible. He told me that after meeting this lady, one of the doctors asked, 'If this lady is so sure she is going to heaven, what is it that's keeping her from just pulling the plug and ending it all? Why is she so keen to stick around, given her poor quality of life, when you consider the paradise she believes she is going to?'

That's a big question. When Mike recounted this story to me, he threw the question my way: 'If heaven is so good and you're all sure you're going there, why aren't more Christians in a hurry to commit suicide?' I was at a bit of a loss as to how to answer him. I knew that Jesus doesn't want us to commit suicide, but actually why? If he has saved me from my sins and my eternal destiny is now to leave this Earth and ascend to heaven, why is it so important for me to hang around here awaiting my inevitable death and my exciting rebirth? In horror, I wondered if I'd discovered some great logical contradiction at the heart of the Christian faith. Why don't we all just commit suicide and go to paradise? I was unable to give Mike much of an answer other than 'Well, Jesus wants me to help people now.' But I still wrestled with this idea. Why is it so important for us to wait on Earth if we're all called to heaven in the end?

The answer to this is entirely tied up in the concept of the kingdom of God. The idea that once saved we are all waiting on Earth to die and go to heaven completely misunderstands the kingdom of God and Jesus' gospel. If we truly grasp Jesus' gospel, then Earth is not just some departure lounge where we wait before God calls us home. Instead, we are saved to begin building that paradise here on Earth – we are saved to build God's kingdom here and now. That is why this disabled woman didn't just want to pull the plug and leave her earthly existence behind: Jesus still had a vital mission and a purpose for her here.

It seems that sometimes we are so fearful of suggesting that you can earn your salvation if you work hard enough at being good that we fail to communicate this. The worry is that by saying to someone, 'You're saved *in order* to build God's kingdom', the message that we communicate is: 'You're saved *by* building God's kingdom.'

This is understandable, and it is vitally important that we don't stray into preaching a version of the gospel that is not centred on God's grace. But this doesn't excuse the fact that, to a certain extent, we're not telling the whole story. Repentance and the forgiveness of sins are at the heart of the gospel message; it must never be anything less than that. But the gospel is also so much more.

By taking away the kingdom of God, we narrow the gospel down to such an extent that, as a church, we forget that Jesus is returning to restore creation and bring in his kingdom, and that we have a great purpose as a church in the interim. We finish the story prematurely, and by doing that we actually miss out on the best bit. The great hope of Jesus' gospel is not only that we have had our sins forgiven and can be in a relationship with God, but that the kingdom of God arrived in Jesus' person and when he returns he will bring it in fully. That is the message that Jesus preached, and that is the transformative message that we should cling to as a church.

THE SELFISH GOSPEL

Whether intentionally or not, what this altered message really boils down to is that we've made the gospel selfish. We have taken on the attitude of our individualistic culture and looked at the gospel through that lens. Our gospel is all about what God has done for us, how much he loves us, how he died for us, how he's given us the gift of eternal life and how he wants a relationship with us. We've taken out the tricky bit. We've taken out the bit where we have to do something in return, the part where we dedicate ourselves to being a follower of Christ and establishing his kingdom. And yet this is what Christ asks of us (Matthew 16:24–25, esv):

> Then Jesus told his disciples, 'If anyone would come after me,
> let him deny himself and take up his cross and follow me. For
> whoever would save his life will lose it, but whoever loses his
> life for my sake will find it.'

In this verse Jesus tells us that if we wish to follow him, and
therefore build his kingdom, we must lose our lives for his sake.
The kingdom of God never advances without sacrifice. But we
don't seem to preach the need to lose our lives as part of our
gospel. And though the idea of sacrifice might be scary, it's actually
the best bit.

Our whole gospel message now screams, 'This is what God can
do for you – it's completely free'! And of course the good news
of the gospel is that it *is* completely free, completely undeserved
and completely gracious. But to become a Christian as we were,
without starting to lose ourselves in Christ, we miss out on half the
story. It's like pausing an action film before we reach the final battle
scene – and that's the most interesting bit of the film.

I think somewhere along the way we decided to shape our gospel
to appeal to our culture – a culture that is trained to think of
ourselves first. We present the gospel as free, easy and attractive –
like it's a hot new product or a new fad diet. Perhaps because we
are afraid it might put people off, we limit the demands of our
gospel so that it doesn't ask for anything past the act of repentance
– we sometimes try to make it seem effortless.

Maybe that seems like a smart marketing strategy given the nature
of our culture, but by narrowing the demands of the gospel, we

have also lost the riches it offers us. It's almost like we have been convinced to buy the product, but a number of us have been left without the instructions. When Jesus asks us to lose our life for his sake, yes it is scary, yes it is a huge commitment – but it is only by losing our lives that we gain all that he has to offer us. It's only when we lay down our lives that we truly step into his kingdom and the incredible opportunity that it presents to us. It's only when we do this that we fully grasp that amazing gift that we have been given and begin to transform ourselves and our culture around us.

I think of it like this. If you study architecture at university, you aren't just getting a degree; you're being apprenticed in a vocation. If you were at the same university doing a different course, perhaps physics, you would graduate with a degree that offers wider possibilities. Yes, many physics graduates go on to become physics academics and scientists, but others will take that degree and go into business or management. Others might end up in a career that has no relation to their degrees at all.

But for the vast majority of those studying architecture, this isn't the case. They study for seven years, and when they graduate they aren't just given a degree, they're smoothly transitioned into a job and a way of life. Their degree is the gateway into a very specific career: that of an architect. Very few people get seven-year architecture degrees and decide to become bankers.

When we become a Christian, it's more like getting a degree in architecture than getting a degree in physics. We graduate from university by giving our lives to Christ and then are instantly enrolled in a way of life – this qualification is supposed to affect all that we are for the rest of our lives. We become disciples of Christ, we work to build his kingdom everywhere that we go and we teach this truth to anyone with a receptive heart.

The problem is, for many of us, although we've graduated with a degree in architecture, we're treating it like a degree in physics. It's like we don't realize that this degree that we have been given is supposed to be a vocation that affects our entire way of life – instead we simply do what we want with our new degree. We use it only as much as it suits us. Some of us may do very little with it, some of us may do other things with it, but many of us don't realize that there's a whole amazing architectural career out there waiting for us if we just use this degree that we've been given.

You surely wouldn't knowingly study as an architect for seven years and then do something completely different with your life, because you're missing the whole point of the degree. But when we understand a selfish gospel, we do exactly that. We accept Jesus as Saviour but fail to step into the kingdom. That means we don't enjoy its benefits; we don't experience the restoration and reconciliation that God's kingdom offers us. We are stuck living the way we were before we were saved. We miss the best part of the story.

HOW THIS CAUSES OUR PROBLEMS

Preaching a selfish gospel isn't just the story that we tell to new Christians. It's the core attitude at the heart of our church culture. The gospel is the heart of the church and the church is the living embodiment of the gospel. Because of this, everything that we are flows from this one story. It is the crux of our identity. And if the gospel that we believe is this distorted, selfish version that is all about the individual, then that means that our attitude as a church is similarly distorted. It's not just that new Christians miss out on the kingdom of God; we all end up missing out.

Theologians use the words 'justification' and 'sanctification' to describe what happens when we are saved. As Christians, we understand that we are justified (saved from our sins) through grace. 'Grace' is defined in the dictionary as 'the free and unmerited favour of God'. And so as followers of Christ, we understand it is by God's amazing mercy that he gave us this unearned, beautiful gift of eternal life and relationship with him. It's a free gift and there's nothing we could do to be worthy of it. But we also believe that once we are 'justified', we are compelled to be 'sanctified'. To go back to our dictionary, 'sanctify' is defined as 'set apart as or declare holy'. What I mean when I say that we are 'compelled to be sanctified' is that once we're saved by Jesus, we can be transformed. God takes us from the broken mess that we find ourselves in and he restores us to his perfect will through the power of his Holy Spirit. His kingdom is built in each of our lives as they start to line up with his perfect plan for us – and as this happens we experience the true satisfaction and wholeness that the gospel offers us. That's not to say it should all be easy when we become a Christian, but it does mean that we move on from where we are now towards God's perfect and pleasing will, and God walks with us on that journey.

So as we are transformed (or sanctified), God builds his kingdom in our lives and uses us to build his kingdom in the lives of those around us. That transformation only happens through sacrifice –

through the hard work of discipleship, giving up ourselves in order to serve God and to serve others as we build God's kingdom – but that sacrifice is ultimately rewarding. Life in all its fullness is only experienced as we let God build his kingdom in us.

However, when we understand a selfish gospel, we disconnect the need to repent of our sins and step into relationship with God from the beautiful restoration that Jesus offers us through his kingdom. A theologian would say that we understand the need to be justified but we aren't compelled to be sanctified. We separate those two ideas so that we think we can be saved without that compulsion to be transformed. While we *can* be saved and carry on exactly as before (Jesus has already saved us from sin), if we do that, we miss out on the riches that Jesus offers us through his kingdom.

There are no two ways about it; transformation takes effort. It is a work of love, and true love is poured out in sacrifice. We have to choose to engage with that process of transformation and we have to persevere through difficulty. The effort is worthwhile, but that doesn't mean the cost is negligible. And this is where the Selfish Gospel causes problems. Specifically, it sets up two key problems: it robs us of vision and it robs us of motivation.

It robs us of vision. Imagine you're an avid Belieber. Many of you may be wondering what that is. For a long time, I had been convinced that Beliebers were a racial group based in the Far East. It was only recently that someone explained to me that a Belieber is actually an avid fan of Justin Bieber, the teenage Canadian pop 'sensation'. Thankfully I was put right before I wrote this analogy!

Now, imagine you're such a big fan of Justin Bieber that in your spare time you love to dress up like him and sing his songs – you're that cool. But imagine, despite being an avid fan of Justin Bieber, that your parents are missionaries and you have been brought up deep in the Amazon jungle. You don't have an internet connection and your computer is ropey at best. The only photos you have of him are paper copies you picked up on your last visit home five years ago. What's worse is those photos have been all messed up by the humid Amazonian climate so that you can't really make him out any more. And the only songs you have are old versions of his first couple of albums on your dad's five-year-old iPod.

If all that were the case, you would be a fairly awful impersonator because you don't have a clear picture of him to model your impression on. You haven't heard any of his recent music. In fact, you'd probably be the singularly worst Justin Bieber impersonator in the world! No matter how talented a vocalist you are, no matter how beautiful your outfit, if you don't have a clear picture of what he looks like and don't know any of his recent songs, you are going to really struggle to provide a true likeness.

And if we settle for an understanding of the Selfish Gospel – if we do not fully grasp the nature of God's kingdom – we are that Belieber. No matter how eager and committed we are to spiritual discipline and building God's kingdom, if we do not fully understand Jesus' message, then we will be limiting ourselves as to how close we can grow to Jesus' likeness. We will struggle to build his kingdom as we won't fully understand its importance or what it looks like.

Now, this is a flawed analogy because, of course, it is not through our own effort that we build God's kingdom and become more Christ-like, but through the power of the Holy Spirit. And of course the Holy Spirit can work outside of our understanding and transform us even if we do not have a full grasp of the true nature of Christ. But I would suggest that it is significantly harder for us to model Christ, grow as his disciples and build his kingdom if we do not fully grasp all that Jesus taught. It is like shooting for a target that we cannot see, or striving for a goal that we do not know.

The second problem is it robs us of motivation. If we accept a selfish gospel then we have no great motivation to engage with a discipled, sacrificial lifestyle. We have no motivation to be transformed further than we feel like at any given time of day. As we read earlier, Jesus asks us to give up everything to follow him, but we rarely preach the need to do that. Instead our Selfish Gospel is watered down to the point where it is only about what God can do for us. We rarely ask people to make that sacrifice. Instead, sometimes the questions we find ourselves asking as we engage with our faith are, 'How will this benefit me?' and 'How much will it cost me?' And when we're feeling exhausted, hungry or broke, we find the answers to those questions seem to be 'It won't' and 'Too much', so we are put off making the sacrifices required to truly become more Christ-like and build his kingdom.

Building sacrifice into our outlook and lifestyle takes time; we need to be supported through it by a community of like-minded Christians. However, more than anything else, we have to *choose* it. If, because of our Selfish Gospel, no-one ever asks us to choose to sacrifice of ourselves, then we're never going to do it. It's simple.

You can't choose to do something if you don't realize it's an option. And if we don't realize that sacrifice is par for the course, it is only logical that we will lack motivation to do it.

From a selfish perspective, sacrificing of ourselves is very silly – it means we go without so that someone else can have more. If we are installed with what the famous ethologist Richard Dawkins calls 'the Selfish Gene' and live our gospel through the selfish attitude of our culture, then sacrifice becomes a really insane thing to do. Once sacrifice starts to look 'insane', it is little wonder that we end up lacking the motivation to engage with it.

The lack of vision and motivation to grow a sacrificial heart is seriously damaging as we look to be transformed. If Jesus calls us to live a radically sacrificial life and we decide that 'giving' rather than 'getting' isn't for us, it is not surprising that Christian lives and churches become half-hearted, inwardly focused and un-attractive. The Selfish Gospel can be seen as the root cause of the three problems with transformation that we looked at in our first section.

If we do not truly understand what discipleship is in terms of the kingdom of God, and if we lack the motivation needed to make the sacrifices associated with discipleship, we will never engage with that process and we will never be transformed personally. Hence we are delirious disciples who don't fully understand what our faith asks of us in terms of discipleship.

If, as a church, we don't fully understand what God's kingdom is and how it exists for those outside of the church community, and if we lack the motivation needed to get up and take the gospel outside of our four church walls, then our church communities will always default to inward-looking, inward-focused institutions. We will struggle to transform our communities. Hence we have a locked-in church that is very inwardly focused.

Finally, if our churches are full of Christians who aren't transformed and churches that aren't transforming, is it any wonder people lack an interest in the church? If the church itself is not especially different from what's around it, why would you listen to its gospel? Add some poor PR, and it's not surprising that people are often openly disdainful of the church and its message – hence the church is often seen as some sort of modern-day Elephant Man.

For the purpose of our metaphor therefore, we see that 'delirious discipleship', 'locked-in syndrome' and the 'Elephant Man' can be seen as symptoms of one, unified, underlying cause: too many of us (myself included) have accepted and embraced the Selfish Gospel.

CONCLUSION

We have seen that the gospel which some of our church culture now preaches is selfish, focusing more on our 'ticket to heaven' and less on building the kingdom of God through sacrifice here on Earth. Therefore, both as churches and individuals we often lack the motivation to live sacrificially. Even if we have the motivation, our narrow understanding of the gospel robs us of a clear vision for what we are aiming for. And because of this Selfish Gospel, we struggle to build a culture of discipleship, we find that our churches are inwardly focused and we see that our culture finds this expression of the church unattractive.

Thankfully though, the story doesn't end there. The Selfish Gospel is not terminal. As Christians, we always have a cure.

6 **The diagnosis**
The Selfish Gospel at work

ANNE AND GOD'S KINGDOM

Now we have an idea of the underlying cause and how the Selfish Gospel causes problems in theory, it is important to explore the outworkings of this illness in practice. It is only when we look at the Selfish Gospel working in the lives of real people that we fully understand the dangers it carries. More importantly, it is only when we apply our theory to the lives of real people that we see the power of the kingdom of God as the one and only antidote. If we really want to grasp the power and beauty of God's kingdom, then we have to look at the lives of the people who are living in it.

And that brings me to Anne. Her name and the names of others in her story have been changed, but the facts remain the same. Anne is a woman who is living in God's kingdom. When you look at her life, you can see the awesome power of God unfolding to bring her situation into line with his perfect will and purpose so clearly. But to see that, you have to understand what she's been through.

Anne grew up in an abusive home. By the age of thirteen she was addicted to alcohol. By the age of seventeen she had been placed in a bed and breakfast because the situation with her parents was so unstable. At this point she became dependent on unemployment benefits and flirting to fund her alcoholism. She was in a pretty broken place. In her own words, she lived her whole life in fear and low self-esteem, and drank alcohol to take it all away.

At the age of twenty, she met a man called James whom God would use to change the course of her life. James had been sniffing glue since the age of fourteen and was dealing cannabis when he met Anne. But he was also a man of faith and he preached the gospel to her.

Anne gave her life to Christ and was baptized in a bathtub with four others (not all at the same time!). But that didn't mark the end of her troubles. She continued to abuse alcohol until she eventually fell in love with and married James within a year of meeting him. He made it a condition of their marriage that she would transition from alcohol to cannabis, because he felt she was better high rather than drunk.

Despite this promise Anne's difficulty with addiction persisted and the couple were unhappy. After fourteen years and two children together, Anne ended up divorced and in rehab. Although going to rehab seemed a positive step, Anne met and fell in love with Chris there, and together they left the programme prior to completing it.

Anne's addiction issues persisted. Chris was a crack and cocaine addict, and together they stayed in a cycle of addiction. Though

Anne kicked her alcoholism with a twelve-step programme, she replaced her addiction to alcohol with an addiction to Chris. She was dependent on him. Enabling his addiction became her addiction.

Although Anne had been baptized and given her life to Christ, she wasn't living in that freedom. She was still a slave to addiction and low self-esteem. She describes it like this: if her life was a car, she was in the driving seat. Jesus was being stored in the boot. He was never thrown out but she never let him drive. He was like a spare tyre: brought along for the ride until there was an accident – at which point he would be allowed out of the boot to deal with the mess!

As you can imagine, Jesus had other plans. He started chasing after Anne in a real and tangible way. She started attending a 'Mums and Toddlers' group at a local church with her youngest child. There, she made friends with a few of the mums from the church. Meanwhile Chris, who had been brought up a Catholic, had a vision of Christ and was compelled by the Holy Spirit to attend services at that same church. Anne started going along with him and after several months she eventually found herself receiving prayer at the front of the church after a service one day. That was it: Jesus was out of the boot and things started to accelerate (so to speak!) from there.

Within two years, Anne had started a 'Bible in One Year' pro-gramme and began studying *The Purpose Driven Life* by Rick Warren. As she did, God spoke to her through Scripture with incredible power. She was challenged by Psalm 139 and the promises it offers, particularly the idea that God loved her so much that he had given her to the parents he had chosen for her. The idea that God had chosen to put her in an abusive home as a helpless child was hard to bear. She began to rant and rave at God because of the pain she had had to endure. As she raged, God started showing her all of the ways that he had walked with her through the difficulty. As God opened her eyes, something broke in her and she could finally see God as Father. The idea of God as Father had previously made him seem unavailable and scary. It had made Anne feel unwanted. But now she understood what it meant to be the daughter of the King. From that point on, Jesus got into the driving seat. Anne separated from Chris and moved him into a B&B. She got a job and eventually started working as an assistant to the vicar at the church she attended.

The real change, and the true beauty of God's kingdom in Anne's story, doesn't shine through changes to her physical circumstances, but through the changes to her relationships.

FOUR ASPECTS OF GOD'S KINGDOM

To really understand the kingdom of God through Anne's story, and grasp why it is the antidote to the Selfish Gospel, we need to go back to our roots. We need to go back to the Garden of Eden because – whether you believe that story to be literal or metaphorical – it is a picture of humanity without sin, and therefore a picture of God's kingdom unfolding and his perfect will in action.

Developed from ideas expressed in Amy Sherman's book *Kingdom Calling*, if we look at Genesis 2 and 3, we see four key differences between God's perfect world and the world we inhabit today.[15] It might be helpful to consider each of these four aspects individually as we look at God's kingdom in Anne's life and try to appreciate its importance in countering the Selfish Gospel.

RELATIONSHIP WITH GOD

In Genesis, before the fall of mankind, God walked with Adam in the Garden of Eden (Genesis 3:8); that was how intimate their relationship was. Clearly, something has gone fundamentally wrong with this relationship between God and us as humans. For a start, God doesn't physically walk among us any more. Moreover, many people have rejected the concept of God and many of those who do know God aren't necessarily letting him sit in the driving seat.

Anne grew up never knowing God. She became a Christian at twenty, but it took another fifteen years or so before she let God have control of her life and truly be King. Now, she has been transformed! She walks with God daily, she knows him as a Father and lives her life to serve God and build his kingdom. That change is an amazing picture of the kingdom of God. God's kingdom is all about restoring each of us to this right relationship with him.

The importance of this work can't be overemphasized: the pinnacle of God's creation is us as humanity, and the pinnacle of his plan is a restoration of his relationship with us. God wants all of us to accept forgiveness of our sins and enter into right relationship with him.

RELATIONSHIP WITH OURSELVES

In the Garden of Eden, man did not die. There was no sickness or mental or physical ill health. The sin that separated us from God didn't just damage our relationship with him; it also damaged our relationships with ourselves. Such damage often manifests as poor health, lack of peace or lack of hope. Therefore, another aspect of God's kingdom is a restoration of our peace with ourselves. Jesus begins this work in his numerous healing miracles and exorcisms. He also promises this restoration of 'self' in the new heaven and the new Earth where there will be no decaying bodies or disease. But Jesus also brought this into being in a subtler way: it is in relationship with him that Jesus promises peace and life in all its fullness (John 10:10; John 14:2).

Once again, you can see this in the most beautiful way in Anne's life. When I talked to her for this book, she told me that before she knew God as Father, she lived her whole life with fear. Now, because she is in right relationship with God, she knows true freedom and she has experienced the most amazing transformation in her relationship with herself. She has a new identity. She has a purpose. She knows that she is fearfully and wonderfully made, chosen, wanted. She is no longer a slave to low self-esteem. She knows she is equal to any man or woman because she is a child of the Living God. And from a physical health perspective, it is through knowing who God is that she finds the most power in her sobriety programme.

Jesus is the Prince of Peace, and a key component of his kingdom is restoring peace with ourselves through relationship with him.

RELATIONSHIP WITH OTHERS

Adam and Eve had a different relationship from the relationships we have today. They walked unclothed with each other in the Garden of Eden and felt no shame. It wasn't just that they were early adopters of the naturism movement; Adam and Eve were one flesh. Just as they were at peace with themselves, they were at peace with one another. In the Bible, it's not until Cain and Abel that arguments, fighting and jealousy are talked about. A central aspect of God's kingdom is restoring our relationships with each other.

Anne's family life was chaotic and her relationships were broken: not only with James and Chris, but with her two children as well who, for a long time, didn't want anything to do with her. But as she has come into right relationship with God and herself, her family relationships have been transformed. Tragically, James recently died; however, until that time he and Chris would both go to Anne's house for lunch on a Sunday. The two of them had become close friends and both considered Anne one of their best friends. They had both come back to church and were in the process of righting their own relationships with God. Her relationships with her children have also been restored, and they too are coming along to church. One of them is even about to start an internship programme there. They all say that the profound difference in Anne could not be ignored.

God's kingdom is about restoring wholeness to broken relationships, whether family relationships or the relationship of one country with another – when God's kingdom is enacted, people are brought together in unity and completeness.

RELATIONSHIP WITH THE ENVIRONMENT

In the Garden of Eden, Adam and Eve had a profoundly different relationship with their environment from the one which we enjoy today. Adam and Eve were stewards of creation, caring for the Garden, and in return the Garden provided for them (Genesis 2:15–16). When God punishes man after the fall, he says that because of our sin we will have to toil and sweat to graft a living from the Earth (Genesis 3:17–18). So when we talk about God's kingdom restoring our relationship with the environment, we are talking about much more than recycling and using green energy (although it does include those things). God's kingdom is about blessing the environment we inhabit and bringing wholeness and peace to that place.

Before Anne was in right relationship with God, she had been arrested twice for drunk and disorderly behaviour. She brought chaos to her environment. Now, Anne faces every morning with the questions: 'How can I serve God today? How can I bless the places that I walk in and bring God's love there?' She has been transformed from an agent of chaos to an agent of peace in her environment.

ANNE AND THE SELFISH GOSPEL

Can you see the difference that Jesus made in Anne's life when she let him take the driving seat? You can easily split her journey to faith into three separate parts: her time without Jesus, her time with Jesus in the boot and her time with Jesus in the driving seat.

The reason she had that three-stage journey is because of the Selfish Gospel. When Anne first gave her life to Jesus, due to the Selfish Gospel, the idea of forgiveness from sin and relationship with Jesus was decoupled from the kingdom of God and his plan to transform her. She was living under a selfish gospel in which we can be saved from our sins but there is no compulsion to change. It wasn't until years later, when Anne dug deep into Scripture and began to spend more time with God, that she started engaging with that process of transformation and saw God's kingdom built in her life and the lives of those around her.

This isn't how it is meant to be. The good news is all about the kingdom of God! Yes, we repent and enter relationship with Jesus. But as we repent we also step into the kingdom; we begin engaging with that process of restoration and we are therefore transformed. We're not supposed to do repentance without restoration or the gospel without transformation. Yet that is exactly what happened in Anne's life and what happens in so many of our lives.

The kingdom of God is like a beautiful mansion. When we believe a selfish gospel, it's like we've stepped through the front door as we repented of our sins, but have then ended up spending the rest of our lives in the porch. Yes, we're inside the mansion – and I'm sure the porch is lovely – but we're missing out on the incredible riches and wonder that are behind the porch door, all because we do not appreciate the kingdom of God and our call to step into it.

Despite being a Christian, it took years before Anne saw restoration in her life – years stuck in the same patterns of addiction, sin and brokenness. When we understand a selfish gospel, we miss out on so much that God has for us; it robs the gospel of power. Anne saw the gospel as a ticket to heaven rather than the ticket to restoration of her life, because that message is forgotten when we preach a selfish gospel. The Selfish Gospel robbed Anne of vision – understanding what her life could be like if she stepped into God's kingdom – and it robbed her of motivation to walk into it. It left her with the distinct impression that she could give her life to Christ and carry on living as she had before, keeping Jesus in the boot. While we *can* do that as Christians because Jesus has forgiven all our sins, when we do, we miss out on the beautiful restoration that God's kingdom offers us.

If we don't tell people about the kingdom of God when we preach the gospel, then we miss out on what God has for us here and now.

CONCLUSION

In summary, we have seen that this Selfish Gospel causes us to miss out on so much that God has for us. When we understand a selfish gospel, we receive the amazing gift of eternal life, but we miss out on all of the restoration and transformation God wants to do in our lives here and now. As in Anne's life, our misunderstood gospel is robbed of its power to transform, leaving us in a situation where we are saved from sin but left as we were before.

But the story doesn't end there. When it comes to the gospel of Christ, the story never leaves us in the grave.

The cuve

- ☐ Shaking off the delivium
- ☐ Breaking out of locked-in syndrome
- ☐ Rehabilitating the Elephant Man

7 The cure
Shaking off the delirium

BALANCING HOLY TRAYS ON OUR HEADS

Although Jesus is doing amazing things in many of our lives and churches, up until now we have looked predominantly at problems. It is not that I want to be a downer – quite the opposite! But just as in medicine, it is only when we have a firm understanding of the symptoms and underlying cause that we can properly identify the solution. That's what I want to do now. Taking our diagnosis, I want us to start looking at how we can reclaim the riches of God's kingdom for our own lives and the lives of our churches.

First, how do we treat our delirious discipleship? As we've gone through this book, we have seen that too often, because of our Selfish Gospel and poor understanding of the kingdom of God, we don't easily grasp the need to disciple ourselves as builders of the kingdom or understand what that looks like. This leaves us delirious, not truly grasping what we're trying to achieve person-ally as Christians, and lacking the vision and motivation to try. In short, the Selfish Gospel robs us of the riches of discipleship.

If you're anything like me, you've probably tried to be a 'better' Christian because it seems like the 'right thing to do'. When I was growing up and first starting to take an interest in my faith, I remember I used to spend an awful lot of time trying to 'be holy'. I spent an awful lot of time trying to make the choices of a transformed Christian – trying to avoid sinning and generally acting more like Jesus. I remember being intensely preoccupied with the pursuit at the age of fourteen or fifteen. At the start of every week I'd write a list of goals that I intended to achieve that week. Something like:

1 Don't swear.
2 Be more humble.
3 Don't get involved with any gossip during lunch breaks at school.

And then for the rest of the week I'd try my utmost to succeed in these tasks. Some weeks I really would manage them! I'd successfully eliminate swearing from my vocabulary or I'd manage to 'be humbler' (whatever that meant to my fourteen-year-old self). And so the next week I'd set myself a new set of holy tasks: I'd do something that I felt was going to make me a better Christian, such as trying to be more kind or trying not to argue with my sister.

The problem was, as I refocused my mind on the new tasks I'd find the old habits would slip back in. Yes, I wouldn't be arguing with my sister, but I'd find myself starting to swear again. I remember feeling as though my Christian walk was like a tray that I was balancing on the top of my head; I felt that I only had so much room to fit everything in. As I added the saucer of humility to my tray, the milk jug of politeness would be knocked off the other side. I only had so much concentration and willpower. However hard I tried, in some aspect of my life, unholy habits would pop up.

I would hear in talks and read in books that we achieved holiness through the power of the Holy Spirit, in Jesus' strength and not our own. But this seemed like a really abstract concept to me at that time. What was 'Jesus' strength'? How was this supposed to make it easier to be holy? Was Jesus going to pop up and freeze my tongue every time I was about to swear? It is very difficult to 'be a better Christian' if we do not understand the kingdom of God and what this means for discipleship.

PAUL'S INSTRUCTIONS

When we accept Jesus as Saviour and believe in his gospel, he invites us to step into his kingdom. Discipleship is our method of reconciliation and restoration with that kingdom; it is when we engage in a process of discipleship that we are transformed. As we are discipled, Jesus builds his kingdom in our hearts and we start to resemble it more closely. Paul explains this in Romans 12:1–2:

> Therefore, I urge you, brothers and sisters, in view of God's mercy, to offer your bodies as a living sacrifice, holy and pleasing to God – this is your true and proper worship. Do not conform to the pattern of this world, but be transformed by the renewing of your mind.

These are arguably some of the most profound and important verses in all of Paul's letters. Held in these verses is the perfect antidote to our delirium as disciples. To understand them fully, we need to grasp a bit more of the background behind this letter.

Addressing the church in Rome, Paul explains the gospel to a church that he'd never visited but very much longed to meet one day. At the very start of this letter, he deals with selfish attitudes very firmly. In chapter 1, Paul is talking about the human condition and he explains that humanity is in the grip of selfishness. He calls this our 'sinful desires', or 'desires of the flesh'. Paul explains that because of our rebellion against God and our worship of things that God has created rather than God himself, God gave us over to our desires. Paul says that we have become enslaved to these desires – forced constantly to please ourselves and look to satisfy ourselves first and foremost.

Then Paul goes on to explain the gospel in the rest of his letter, examining how God's mercy means that we can be saved from this state. Paul does not preach a selfish gospel; he preaches a full, broad gospel as he explains the importance of the kingdom of God. After explaining this gospel, in Romans 12:1–2 Paul tells us how we are to respond to it. Allow me to paraphrase these verses:

> Therefore, because you believe in the gospel, I urge you as Christians to offer your lives as a living sacrifice; this is how we serve God and build his kingdom. Do not conform to the selfish pattern of this world, but be transformed in discipleship.

Paul's use of the word 'therefore' is like a hinge that the whole of the letter rests on. Paul has spent eleven chapters explaining what the gospel is (including the vital role of the kingdom of God) and then he tells us 'therefore'. It's as if he's saying, 'This is it, this is what happens after we've believed the gospel of God's kingdom.' He links the gospel to the 'renewing of our minds' to show us that sacrifice through discipleship is the only proper response to the gospel. He's telling us that if we truly grasp the kingdom of God, then we are compelled to be transformed, and that transformation occurs through the 'renewing of our minds' in discipleship.

As we engage with a process of discipleship, we make the time and the space to allow the Holy Spirit to transform our hearts and our minds in line with God's will. And as God's kingdom is his perfect will in action, this discipleship allows God to build his kingdom inside us and we are transformed.

When I was younger, I was trying to live a life of holiness without being discipled. I was trying to live out his kingdom without making the space for Jesus to build it within my heart. It was all outward effort rather than inward transformation. When we try to be holy through outward effort, it becomes about our energy levels, how enthusiastic we are to be holy at any given time. But our energy levels will always dip; we will always stumble if that is our method. However, if through discipleship we make space for God to transform us from the inside out, holiness instead becomes the outward manifestation of our inward identity. Rather than holiness being about our effort, we find ourselves becoming more holy because that is simply who we are. God is building his kingdom within us, and that kingdom naturally shines through who we are.

A LIFE OF DISCIPLESHIP - A LIFE OF RELATIONSHIP

That's all well and good, but how do we actually achieve this? Up until now, we've talked a lot about discipleship and spiritual discipline in theory without really sketching out how this all works in the context of our day-to-day lives.

I've mentioned it before, but Tozer's book *The Pursuit of God* is an excellent (and very short) examination of the attitude that must be at the heart of any effort of discipleship and so, if the next section leaves you wanting to take a deeper look at discipleship, this would be an excellent place to start.[16] Foster's *A Celebration of Discipline*, also previously mentioned, is a fantastic discussion of spiritual discipline – though perhaps a little heavier and so it may take some time.[17] Finally, Pastor Mike Breen and global leadership movement 3DM have produced an excellent book called *Building a Discipling Culture* that looks at how to build a culture of discipleship.[18] That said, although the book you have in your hands isn't a manual on how to disciple ourselves, it's worth taking the time to examine some basic principles here.

In chapter 1, while discussing the problem the church has in creating not just 'Christians' but disciples, we talked about various spiritual disciplines, as highlighted by Foster in his book. First, the personal disciplines of praying, studying Scripture, meditating on Scripture and fasting. Second, the corporate disciplines of confession, worship, guidance and celebration. And finally, the outward disciplines of simplicity, solitude, submission and service. While we don't have time to discuss each of these in depth now, we can consider the attitude that underpins them and briefly look at some practical approaches we can adopt.

Let's start with the attitude. If the Christian faith were a romantic relationship, then the moment we choose discipleship is the moment we move past casual flirting and chance encounters, and formalize our romantic interest into something more concrete. If you like, discipleship is the beginning of the dating process. Jesus is no longer someone who we bump into on a Sunday or have the odd conversation with as and when we have a spare moment; he is someone that we choose to make the space to spend time with. Just like any formalized relationship, discipleship requires a desire on our behalf to enter that relationship. A disciple is a person who has fallen so in love with Jesus that even though the heady rush of first romance may have faded, he or she still chooses to sacrifice himself or herself in becoming more like Jesus. It requires commitment on our behalf to thrive. And naturally, like every relationship that we will ever have, it will change us.

We've seen that transforming relationships is an inherently connected process. When we are getting to know a loved one, it is only when we grasp the potential of our relationship with that person that we seek to spend time becoming the best version of ourselves for him or her. And it is only when we become the best version of ourselves for him or her that we see the potential of that relationship come into being. Similarly, it is only when we grasp the kingdom of God that we see the need to be transformed through discipleship. And it is only when we are transformed through discipleship that we will begin to build the kingdom of God here on Earth. In this way, each of the spiritual disciplines provides a different way to invest in our relationship with God. Each of these disciplines is an effort of love that, over time, acts to transform us as it reflects God's love back onto us. And the best part? Jesus is already 'all in'. The heart of the gospel is relationship. The whole of our history centres on the fact that God desires relationship with humanity, the pinnacle of creation.

MARINATING AND REFLECTING

Discipleship is a process in which we could be said to be marinating in God's love. Just as a marinating joint takes on the flavour of the marinade it sits in, as we let God's love cover and saturate us, we take on the nature of that love. As I mentioned at the beginning of our diagnosis, discipleship is the process of becoming who Jesus would be if he were us. Just as a joint of meat retains its nature in a marinade, we also retain our 'self-ness' as we grow in Christ. But over time, a joint also takes on the flavour of the marinade until the whole joint resonates and bursts with that flavour. As we are discipled, we retain our 'self-ness' but we also begin to resonate with God's love so much that it bursts forth from our very core. This is what discipleship is all about: investing in Jesus in order to be transformed by the Holy Spirit so that we too resonate with the Father's love.

The key to all spiritual disciplines is reflection. Soaking in God's love, letting it season us, then examining ourselves to find the areas that are not consistent with the flavour of the marinade – the areas of ourselves that are not in line with God's kingdom. When we find those areas, we are then compelled to engage in a transformational process and invite the Holy Spirit to change us. It may seem obvious, but to engage in this process of discipleship, we need to make space within our daily lives to practise the spiritual disciplines. As we invest in our relationship with Jesus through these disciplines, they act as the structure which guides us through this transformational process.

Over the next few pages therefore, we are going to consider the practical aspects of the personal disciplines of prayer, reading the Bible, fasting and meditating, and see how they lead to the transformation of our identity.

REACHING NEW DEPTHS IN PRAYER

For many of us, myself included, our prayers centre around our own immediate wants and needs. We pray about stresses and strains on our minds, and ask God to act in situations that concern us in our lives. Of course, these prayers are welcomed by God with open ears and open arms, but he also invites us to pray prayers that shift our focus further, wider and bigger than our immediate wants and needs.

God invites us to pray prayers of thankfulness and praise, prayers that describe all that he is and all that he has done for us. He wants us to praise his incredible character of love and compassion, his amazing actions in human history to save and redeem us, and his awesome power and authority. When we spend time praying such prayers, they can have two effects on us. First, they make our faith bigger; second, these prayers help to make our 'self' smaller – that is to say, they act to humble us.

FAITH, HUMILITY AND OBEDIENCE

Faith, humility and obedience are three sides of the same triangle. It is possible but rare to find one of the three without also finding the other two.

Humility is the acknowledgment of our self's true position in the universe and before God. It is the understanding that we are only a tiny part of the universe and completely powerless before God. When we are completely humbled, we become aware that every breath that we breathe is a gift from God, which, if he willed, could be taken away in an instant. Coming to that realization requires an acknowledgment of both our own weakness and God's unfathomable strength. In order to be truly humbled, we have to understand that we are incredibly powerless and ultimately helpless before God, at the same time as grasping that God is all-powerful and in total control.

A few weeks ago, I went surfing for the first time in a couple of years. I found the whole process absolutely exhausting and, you guessed it, humbling. Having taken much longer than I'd wanted paddling myself into the correct position, I waited for a wave to build. As the first wave arrived, I paddled hard and managed to catch it, but as I popped up on my board, I realized how big the wave was – much bigger than I had thought! I freaked out. Rather than successfully standing up and surfing my way along the face of the wave, I panicked, slipped off my board and got hammered by the full weight of the wave. It drove me down into the sea, turning me head over heels again and again. I was completely powerless to resist its force. When my world finally stopped spinning, I began to swim to the surface, but I suddenly realized how deep I was – perhaps ten feet down – and how much force the wave must have smashed me with. As I broke the surface and clambered back onto my board, I felt completely humbled. Before that wave I'd forgotten how heavy the waves are and how easily they can throw my body around. I realized how powerful the sea is and how helpless I am before that power.

Now, praying to God prompts a range of emotions. Sometimes (like me in the waves) we can be shocked and indeed terrified by what God stirs within us. Other times, we can be comforted, embraced, healed or even amused in God's presence. However, no matter what the emotion, more often than not when we come to God with praise and thanksgiving, we will usually find ourselves becoming humbled.

When we pray prayers that look past our lives in the here and now, we begin to grasp how powerful and wonderful God is, and how helpless we are before him. As we focus our minds on worshipping God in prayer, he gifts us with a renewed understanding of our position in the world in relation to his. And as our understanding of that truth grows, we find that it is not just our humility which grows, but also our faith. It is very difficult for us to grow in our understanding of God's awesome power without finding our faith in that power also growing.

I was doing some medical research a few years ago with an eminent professor. The research opportunity had fallen into my lap in an incredibly fortuitous way and I hadn't really grasped quite how eminent this professor really was. However, as I began to read around the subject in preparation, I realized that this professor's name was on all of the best papers that I was reading. Her name was everywhere! Not only was I completely humbled to be working with her, I also began to have a lot more faith that the research that I was doing under her was going to go somewhere. I realized that she was a scientist who frequently published research, and so my research had a much greater chance of being published too.

In a similar way, as we pray prayers of thankfulness and praise, our faith and our humility grow because we realize that all of our talents, achievements and wealth ultimately result from God's amazing mercy and grace. And when we realize that, we are humbled beyond measure. What's more, we realize that not only is God able to do immeasurably more than we could ask or imagine, but he is also willing.

And as God grows our humility in our small selves and our faith in him, our great God, we find that the last side of our 'faith, humility, obedience' triangle falls into place. Obedience is simply humility in practice; when we are humbled before God, it leads us to submit to him and therefore obey him. If we truly understand who God is and have faith in him, and if we grasp who we are and how helpless we are, submitting to God's authority becomes a very logical next step.

To go back to my experience doing research with the eminent professor, as I began to realize how incredible this professor was, I found myself hanging off her every word. Don't get me wrong, I was already trying to do what she asked of me, but when I realized that she was a real leader in the field, I was prepared to do anything that she asked of me, however much effort it might require. Because of her status, I trusted her judgment so much. I submitted myself to her authority and strove to do exactly as she asked. My submission to her was a natural product of the new-found humility I had before her and my faith in her abilities.

As we reflect on our lives in thankfulness and praise, not only do our faith, humility and obedience increase, but God also brings to mind new areas where we need to submit to him – often areas we were never aware of before.

It's a little like this. When I was at school, I always thought I was quite good at rugby. But when I got to university, that changed. I realized I was an awful player! Looking back, this shock (though still regrettable) is somewhat understandable. At school we had been asked to perform to a much lower standard and played against schools of similar ability levels. I was the archetypal big fish in a small pond. When I got to university, I was in a much bigger pond and I found myself surrounded by much better rugby players. I became aware of inadequacies in my rugby game that I had never even realized before.

In a similar way, when we draw close to our immeasurably strong God in prayer, he makes us more aware of ourselves and our weakness. As we gain these new insights, we become aware of things in us that need to change. The Holy Spirit brings to mind aspects of our character, persistent habits and sinful actions that are not in line with his love. As we marinate ourselves in that love, we find that he compels us to submit those things to him so that in those areas we obey him – he shows us how to become more loving and how to serve him – hence our behaviour changes and we are transformed. By highlighting the areas in our life that need to change, God is not being pushy or cruel. Like with a clinically overweight patient, God is calling us to shape up so that we can run, and dance, and celebrate with ease and energy. He is calling us to lose anything that is holding us back from living our lives to the full.

WHAT ABOUT STUDYING SCRIPTURE?

The Bible is the story of God's relationship with humanity, and as we study and reflect on it the Holy Spirit also leads us on a transformational journey.

When we study the Bible, the Holy Spirit reveals so much of his loving character to us and we become more aware of God and who he is. He also shows us similarities (or differences) between ourselves and many of the characters in the Bible, and so we reach a greater understanding of who we are, our weakness and the strength that God provides. Just as the discipline of prayer leads us into new realizations of who God is and who we are, causing our faith, humility and obedience to grow, the discipline of studying Scripture leads us on the same journey, just by a different route. As we reflect on Scripture, we learn more about ourselves and more about God. This humbles us, grows our faith and causes us to repent and seek a renewed spirit of obedience. As the Bible tells us, the Holy Spirit helps to lead us in repentance. Through his strength, we are empowered to become more like Jesus. There are many ways to study Scripture, but it is always good to start by praying for God to speak to us through it. It is also a good idea to end with a response to what we have read, whether that be through prayer or journaling.

You might not always be prompted to respond in this way; the Bible is a wonderfully varied book, which will prompt a wonderfully varied response. But the only way to discover the many things it will make you think and feel is to open its pages and have a go.

FASTING

Fasting is the discipline of withholding something from ourselves for a period of time in order to honour God and draw closer to him. The classic example of fasting is to fast from food; this might involve withholding all food and liquids (other than water) for any time ranging from a few hours to a few days. This can be very challenging and rewarding, but it also takes training and practice to fast from food for periods longer than a day or so – it is actually quite dangerous to try to fast from food for long periods suddenly and without previous practice.

Although fasting is often associated with food, you can actually fast from almost anything. You can fast from anything that you will miss if it's not freely available, whether that be television programmes, mobile phones and computers, or even work!

Fasting does many wonderful things for us; it illuminates our reflections. Whatever we are fasting from, as we find ourselves missing it we are reminded how dependent we are on that thing and how important it is for us. We also come to the realization that that thing is a gift from God, given to us because of his grace. In this way, as we fast we grasp a deeper understanding of God's character of mercy and also of our dependence on him. This leads us on the same path of increasing humility, faith and obedience-through-repentance outlined above.

MEDITATION

Much like studying the Bible and praying, there are many different
ways to meditate. When we think of meditation, we often think of
Eastern spiritualism, which teaches that meditation is a technique
to empty one's mind. In Christianity, rather than trying to empty
our minds, we meditate to fill our minds with God. If we meditate
on Scripture, we achieve this through focusing our thoughts on a
certain passage.

For example, let's use Psalm 28:7: 'The LORD is my strength and my
shield', and work our way through it.

First of all, we focus on God. We put aside any other thoughts and
concerns that may be shooting around in our heads and focus our
thoughts on God. Then, once we are ready to begin, we start to
pick apart Scripture into words, or collections of words, and think
about what each of those words means for us.

Using Psalm 28:7, we could begin with the words 'The LORD is'.
We ask ourselves what this means to us right now. We could ask
questions like: 'Who is God? Who is he to me right now? Who
does Scripture say that God is? How has God demonstrated that
to me over the last day/week/year/lifetime?' As we chew over
questions like these, we let our answers start to form prayers; we
begin to praise God for who he is and what he has done for us.

The next phrase we could consider is 'my strength'. Again, we ask
ourselves what that means to us. We may ask questions like: 'Where
do I find my strength? How strong do I feel?' And again, as we

consider these questions, we let our answers form into prayers, asking God to strengthen us where we feel weak and thanking him for areas of strength in our life.

Then we can consider the two phrases together: 'The LORD is my strength.' Again we ask ourselves what that means, and questions we ask may include: 'Is God really my strength? What other things may be fulfilling that role in my life right now? How has God strengthened me recently?'

Then we turn our attention to the phrase 'my shield'. Again we may ask questions about what things we use to protect or hide ourselves; we ask ourselves if there are areas we need sanctuary in right now. As we find answers to these questions, we reflect them back in prayer. Then we could consider the phrase, 'The LORD is my shield', asking similar questions which flow into prayer again, before finally considering the phrase, 'The LORD is my strength and my shield', and repeating the process of contemplation leading to prayer.

By using this simple verse, you can see how we can begin a journey of transformation. We've asked deep questions that have helped us to reflect on who we are and who God is. Through these questions we have learned more about ourselves and about God – God will have been growing our humility and our faith. These qualities will lead us into new obedience, through a process of repentance, and hence to transformation.

Now, this process of meditation, or personal discipline more generally, is not a quick process. In our instant culture we expect sudden results and dramatic change. That isn't how the spiritual disciplines work, and that is why many of us find them so difficult. But we do change, slowly but surely, and the changes that we undergo can last a lifetime.

DISCIPLESHIP IS A LIFESTYLE FOUNDED IN RELATIONSHIP

If each of us could carve out thirty minutes a day to invest time in our relationship with Jesus and find some space to fast from things every couple of weeks, I guarantee that we would change. It might take six months but we would change irrevocably; we would become more like Jesus in ways that we didn't realize needed to change! A great way to measure this change is through journaling: writing a little every day or two, just noting where we are with God and what we feel God is working on in us. As time passes we can review these little notes and see the amazing change that God has worked in us and the journey that he has brought us on.

That said, it doesn't take long to work out that discipleship is about more than just thirty minutes a day. Discipleship is a lifestyle. The spiritual disciplines are vital to that lifestyle, but they are far from the end of it. Discipleship is about taking that reflectional journey and making it our every thought. Discipleship is living in such a way that we are constantly reflecting on ourselves in the light of God's love and being transformed into his likeness. When we are truly engaged in a process of discipleship, we are taking all of our thoughts, actions and words captive, examining them in the light of the Holy Spirit and the truth of Scripture, and then bending and shaping them until they all resonate deeply with God's love. It's a constant process that we engage in every minute of every day.

When I was a student, I found myself in surgery with a senior doctor; it was the weekend so there weren't many doctors around. This meant that he and I were the only doctors (or doctors-in-training, in my case!) in the theatre. For want of a more experienced pair of hands, it fell to me to assist. As the senior doctor was performing the operation and doing all the hard work, I was being an extra set of hands when he needed them: helping to keep the incision open, cutting the stitches at the appropriate time and so on. The problem was, I had never seen this operation before, and with the surgeon not really communicating very much, I was never sure what I was supposed to be doing. He just gestured with his head or his hand when he wanted me to perform a certain task, without telling me what that task was or how I was supposed to do it. I was expected just to know what he wanted of me – but I didn't!

Perhaps understandably, the senior doctor was getting quite frustrated by my consistent failure to keep up with him. In the end he exclaimed, 'When you're assisting a surgeon in theatre, you really need to know the operation so well that as you see the surgeon's hands move you know instinctively what he wants you to do.' I gulped and thought to myself, 'Well that's great, but I only met you this morning, I've never seen this operation before and understanding more than the basic principles of certain operations is something you learn after medical school!' However, I knew better than to argue. I decided just to keep quiet and try harder.

Now, I appreciate that this senior doctor had more pressing issues at hand, but had someone shown me what I needed to learn, or, better still, walked me through the operation, I would have more closely resembled the senior doctor in my instinctive actions. And the same can be said of a lifestyle of discipleship: it works best in relationship. Discipleship works best when there is someone alongside us, not tutting when we fall short of their expectations, but spurring us on. As a church, we should be a community of disciples aiming to build God's kingdom in the world around us – but we should also have a couple of close friends around ourselves who spur us on more closely.

The youth ministry Urban Saints has an incredible initiative called 'Live Life 123' that aims to encourage people to live within this culture of discipleship.[19] They're passionate about doing that because they understand that a life of discipleship is the path to transformation. Furthermore, they are quick to note that discipleship doesn't happen in isolation.

Many people find it helpful to have someone who is a little further along their walk with Christ leading them through their own process of transformation. For many, if not most people, having that spiritually mature person to look up to and lean on is helpful in a number of ways. As we mature and God's kingdom grows in us, we can look to take the hands of others on this journey and provide that same voice of maturity that we have speaking into our lives.

CONCLUSION

Earlier in this book, we saw how, too often, we have become delirious as disciples – we've forgotten what it means to be a true disciple of Jesus. Next, we identified the root cause: many of us have understood a selfish gospel, meaning we are forgiven and saved, but fail to grasp the kingdom of God and the heart of sacrificial living and transformation that this calls us to here and now. Diagnosis in hand, in this chapter we have started to push back against our Selfish Gospel and treat our discipleship delirium.

Rejecting our Selfish Gospel and accepting Jesus' message in full, we have seen how transformation is the only logical response to the gospel. This starts with a transformation of identity: as we submit to Christ, we let him build his kingdom in our hearts and, in turn, become more like him. This transformation is achieved through discipleship, grasping the proper attitude and engaging in the practicalities of the spiritual disciplines such as prayer and studying Scripture.

One symptom treated; two more to go.

8 The cure
Breaking out of locked-in syndrome

HOW TO TRANSFORM OUR CULTURE

I remember feeling so out of place it was horrible! I understood what it was like to hope the ground opened up and swallowed me whole. I have rarely felt so intensely uncomfortable doing something as simple as standing in a room.

I was in Australia. I had travelled there after medical school to study in the local A&E, before I started work in the UK. While I was there, I stumbled upon this church that met in a school sports arena. It had all started so brightly: I had arrived at the campus where it was held, I had gone through the entrance doors and the welcomers had smiled at me and shaken my hand. But then I found myself thrust through the welcome tunnel and into the bowels of the church.

People were standing about, milling around and discussing the goings-on of church life. This church didn't serve refreshments before the service and, perhaps in the naïve hope of cake, I had timed my arrival fifteen minutes before the service began. Cake-less, I just stood there awkwardly in the corner with my hands in my pockets, for fifteen long minutes, feeling intensely unwelcome. It was like I was an intruder in a private place. It wasn't about the lack of cake (well, not entirely), and it wasn't that anyone was rude to me; the problem was no-one came and spoke to me at all. A few people looked at me quizzically – a foreign being in their familiar place – but that only made it worse; their looks only made me feel more self-conscious.

I honestly can't remember the last time I felt that out of place. And I'm a guy that has grown up in the church and been around Christians all my life. I'm pretty comfortable with how churches work. In that moment it was like I was trapped in a room with the locked-in church body. Someone might flicker an eyelid in my direction as they mentally questioned what I was doing there, but on the whole, people were paralysed in their efforts to interact with me.

Now, to their credit, this church did 'officially welcome' me after the service; they took me to a special table and gave me a pack to take home with me (there was even a free pen inside!) and after they had done that, some people did come up and talk to me. But prior to that after-service experience, I felt distinctly uncomfortable.

This was arguably an example of the Selfish Gospel at work – not specifically in the people themselves, but in the inward-focused culture within which they operated. Understanding a selfish gospel promotes the idea that once we are saved, this is the end of the gospel story. If our understanding of the gospel ends once we are saved, it is no wonder that we have no compulsion to look outside of our church circle – or interact with the strange new person in our church space (until they are 'officially welcomed', of course!).

We may appreciate a call to evangelize, but in our Selfish Gospel attitude, evangelism is limited to a process of convincing other people to agree with us. Without an understanding of the kingdom of God – a kingdom which exists to serve those who are not yet a part of it – we struggle for motivation and vision for a broader programme of restoration and transformation. We don't grasp that Jesus saved us and invited us to build his kingdom with him, to take our broken world and help transform it so that it better represents God's perfect loving will. If we do not grasp that this is the vision for our lives once we are saved, we don't really have a motivation to start building that kingdom. The kingdom of God never advances without sacrifice, and if we think the story has already ended with our personal salvation, where is the motivation to make difficult and painful sacrifices regardless of whether they are actually what is best for us?

The good news is, as we grasp a broader gospel, we are compelled to engage with this programme. We have just spent a chapter looking at how, if we engage with discipleship, we will become more like Jesus and his kingdom will grow in us. The next step is that as God's kingdom grows in our hearts, we will start to see it grow around us.

Kris Vallotton says, 'The Invisible Kingdom inside a person ultimately becomes the Visible Kingdom around them.'[20] That means we transform the reality around ourselves, slowly but surely, so that it becomes more like the reality within ourselves. In essence, people who are peaceful ultimately create peace around themselves. People who are bitter and angry create bitterness and anger. As God's kingdom grows in us, it is only natural that it begins to spill out and grow in the world around us too, through the power of the Holy Spirit. But this transformation will only happen as we engage with those people and places that are not currently aligning with God's kingdom.

Similar to our last chapter, this is a huge topic that we can only hope to skim the surface of here. Writer and academic Amy Sherman has written a fantastic book called *Kingdom Calling*, which provides an in-depth, practical look at how we can really be equipped to build God's kingdom in our everyday lives.[21] Dr Sherman's work has inspired a lot of the suggestions I'm about to make, and provides a much more detailed vision for how we can be equipped to build God's kingdom. However, for the purposes of our kingdom treatment, we are going to take a much briefer look at how we can embrace the authority that Jesus gives us to transform our culture.

The crux of the matter is that we cannot begin to transform our culture until we have started to transform ourselves. We have to start with discipleship, letting God's kingdom grow in us. Only as we mature with God do we become ready to daily build his kingdom in the environment around us. If we are not intimate with God, we will never manage to get into rhythm with him, and consequently we will always struggle to see or take opportunities to build his kingdom.

THE KINGDOM OF GOD IS DEFINED BY SACRIFICE

In our locked-in churches, we seem to be particularly poor at building God's kingdom outside of our church communities. But that isn't how it's supposed to be, as Jesus tells us very clearly in Mark.

In Mark's Gospel, the question on everyone's lips is: 'Who is Jesus?' It is a question that echoes throughout Mark's narrative and it is even posed by his disciples. Despite being his closest friends and followers, they cannot understand who Jesus is or what his exact mission is about. In chapters 8–10, Jesus seeks to establish the nature of his mission very firmly in their minds in a series of three teaching episodes (Mark 8:27–38; 9:30–37 and 10:32–45).

In each of these episodes, the disciples have a misunderstanding; they say something or behave in a way that shows they do not grasp the true nature of Jesus' kingdom or his mission. Actually, in each of these episodes they behave in a way that betrays their selfishness. Every time they do this, Jesus firmly rebuts their misunderstanding with explanations that show his true calling and the sacrificial nature of his kingdom.

In the final of these three episodes, in Mark 10:32–45, James and John come to Jesus and ask to be seated by his right and left hand in his new kingdom. These were the positions of honour, power and authority in their culture – so really they're asking to be honoured and given authority over all others. Jesus reprimands them gently but firmly for their misunderstanding. Here is what he says to the gathered disciples:

> You know that those who are regarded as rulers of the
> Gentiles lord it over them, and their high officials exercise
> authority over them. Not so with you. Instead, whoever
> wants to become great among you must be your servant, and
> whoever wants to be first must be slave of all. For even the
> Son of Man did not come to be served, but to serve, and to
> give his life as a ransom for many.

In this pivotal teaching episode, Jesus tells the disciples in no
uncertain terms that if they want to be great in his kingdom, they
must become the servant of all – not just the other disciples, but
everyone. He suggests that it is in service that we find greatness in
Jesus' kingdom, rather than in the positions of power and authority
as in human kingdoms. He is telling James and John directly that if
they want the greatness and the honour, it's not about sitting in a
special seat: it's about sacrificing your life in service of others. And
this should be the model for our churches too. We should seek to
serve not just ourselves or our inward church communities, but
everybody.

In this teaching, Jesus even goes so far as to compare the disciples'
mission with his own. When Jesus died on the cross, he did not just
do it for his followers or his friends, he did it for all mankind for
all eternity, so that whoever believes in him could enter his
kingdom and receive the gift of eternal life. But in the passage
above, Jesus compares his own sacrifice with the mission of the
disciples. The implication is clear: our task as Jesus' followers is to
sacrifice ourselves in order to serve our world, just as he did,
whether we are serving members of our church community or not.

MOUNTAIN CLIMBING

But how are we going to do that? It's all well and good saying that we should sacrifice ourselves to build God's kingdom and serve our world, but what does that actually look like? How do we start restoring our communities so that they align with God's pleasing and perfect will?

Just as in our previous chapter, we need to consider the attitude underpinning this task, while also thinking about practical aspects.

Starting with the attitude, if we want to be a church that is empowered to build God's kingdom through sacrifice, the church needs to teach and model a culture where we are encouraged to go and engage with those outside of the church – where we go and build relationship with our (literal) neighbours and local communities. We need to encourage and model a style of church where we are actively encouraged to go out and get involved in social circles outside of the church social circle. And, above all else, we need to encourage and model a style of church in which attendees are encouraged to invest deeply in real relationships with people outside of the church.

I kind of think of it like this. I lived in the borough of Hammersmith and Fulham for eight years, and while I was living there I saw the area go through the most amazing transformation. It went from a relatively normal area with pockets of deprivation to being one of the most exclusive areas in London but still with those same pockets of deprivation. In my first six years in London property prices went up hugely, pushing people from Kensington and

Chelsea further out, often into Fulham, and so the area underwent a rapid redevelopment process. But, at the same time, those people who were living in council-owned housing and those who had lived there all their lives stayed put. This created a situation where one street would have some of the most exclusive addresses in London, and the next street over would have some of the worst deprivation in the city. And these two worlds never interacted. The people living in their beautiful exclusive addresses were oblivious to the poverty on their doorstep.

I always remember hearing a talk by one of the local police chiefs who came to our church to talk about the high crime in the area. He described a lot of the structure of the gangs who would run drugs throughout Fulham. He shared how huge drug deals would take place in cars parked up on exclusive streets in Fulham as wealthy, affluent individuals walked past completely unaware of the criminal underworld that was literally beneath their nose. The two worlds were completely separate – and both wanted to keep it that way. The wealthy residents lived in an affluent bubble where they did not want to interact with the poverty so close to them. They might walk past an area of deprivation or they might see a drug deal in the back of the car, but they didn't realize what they were looking at. They were completely oblivious.

Sometimes, I worry that the church is like that with our culture. Although we inhabit the same geographical location as mainstream culture, and although we may pass through it on our way to the shops with our family or a restaurant with (Christian) friends, socially we remain in that bubble of Christian culture. We may work in an area dominated by mainstream culture, but we are protected by this professional façade that stops us from really living in it. We do not engage with that mainstream culture in a vulnerable or real way, and we struggle to form real or meaningful relationships with those outside our Christian bubble.

A major part of breaking out of the locked-in syndrome is about empowering the church to go and inhabit the world rather than hide from it in the safety of our church buildings. We have to have a culture where it is normal to spend your time engaging with people who aren't in the church. It needs to be taught well by the leaders, modelled well by members and also, particularly in the initial stages, it needs to be supported and encouraged with accountability.

When we spend large portions of our lives with people who don't know Christ, it is like finding ourselves on the frontline of faith: we are in a position carrying the potential for great influence, but we are also left vulnerable to hurt. It is our role as members of the church, the body of Christ, to help and support one another to minimize this risk and maximize our influence as far as possible.

COMFORTABLE LIVING ROOM OR MOUNTAINEERING BASE CAMP?

For many of us at the moment, the church is a central hub that we are encouraged to spend much (if not all) of our free time in. Like a home from home, it's a place of security and safety that we base our lives around. But rather than being a central hub, the church should be like a base camp at the bottom of a mountain. It should exist to equip and enable us to go out and engage with the community around the church. If we're feeling damaged and broken, it is to the base camp that we return for restoration and recuperation, but we return there with the understanding that we are recuperating in order to head back out on the mountain trails when we're ready.

This is actually the model of engagement that we see Jesus using in Mark 6. He sends the disciples out into the world to build his kingdom; then, when their work is accomplished, Jesus leads them on a retreat away from the crowds in order to recuperate and be re-equipped in a place of safety. You'll notice he doesn't retreat up a mountain to begin with and sit with the disciples building an inward-looking (if very holy) community while completely neglecting the world outside. He leads his followers into pockets of quiet to recharge *after* their mission, after they've already been sent out to transform lives and witness the kingdom of God.

Now, just because we want to engage with the community outside of the church, it does not mean that we neglect the community of the church itself. If we do that, then the church ceases to be a community. We need to find a balance. On the one hand the church needs to fulfil its role as a community of restoration and safety for the damaged and broken, and on the other it needs to fulfil its role as equipper and planner of mountain-scaling pursuits. We will look at the practicalities of striking this balance further on in this chapter.

TRANSPORT INFRASTRUCTURE

The second part of the attitude we need to adopt focuses on transport infrastructure. That may sound mad, but bear with me.

When I was studying GCSE geography, I did a brief module on development. In this module we looked at how companies choose where to build factories and how governments try to encourage them to locate in certain areas.

Something that really struck me throughout this module was the emphasis on infrastructure. A company won't just build a factory in any old place; it chooses to build the factory close to local transport links – shipping ports, airports or roads – so that it can ship its products out and raw materials in more easily. That shipping process is essential to the work of the factory. Without it, the factory ceases to be functional because raw materials cannot be delivered to make new products, and products can't be shipped out to sell to buyers.

A company could build the most high-tech, innovative factory in the world, but without effective transport links it would be next to useless. An old factory that has access to its required raw materials is going to be much more useful than a new cutting-edge factory that doesn't, even if that old factory is full of out-of-date equipment.

As a church, we are not too dissimilar to those factories in that we are wholly reliant on our transport infrastructure. We can be a part of the best church in the world, with the most fantastic worship, cutting-edge preaching and powerful prayer ministry, but if we cannot get people who don't know Jesus to connect with our church, then we are factories without access to raw materials. If we are not engaging with communities outside of the church, then how are we going to build God's kingdom there? How can we have a transformative influence on people without a relationship with them?

This is the heart of the matter: if we want to grow the kingdom of God in our world, it is essential that we invest in our transport infrastructure. I'm not suggesting we literally need better roads and bigger car parks around church buildings; what we need to be is Christians who are empowered to grow and build relationships with those who do not yet know Jesus. We need to be a movement with a constant focus on those outside of our community, a movement with a heart to build bridges and invest in those people. They're the 'raw materials', and it's through relationship that we will connect the church with them and begin that process of restoration to God and hence transformation.

PROACTIVE VERSUS REACTIVE KINGDOM BUILDING

Our attitude starts with transport infrastructure, but it doesn't end there. We don't just need to be intentional about getting outside of the church community; we also need to be intentional about putting those kingdom building blocks in place.

As we engage in the process of discipleship, the Holy Spirit transforms us so that we look more like Jesus. We become more loving, more peaceful, more patient, more obedient – Paul talks about these characteristics in Galatians 5:22–23: 'But the fruit of the Spirit is love, joy, peace, patience, kindness, goodness, faithfulness, gentleness [and] self-control' (ESV).

As we become more like Jesus and grow in these qualities, we react to certain situations in ways which are similar to Jesus. In our places of work or study, we feel compelled to build others up, perhaps even as other colleagues are gossiping about them behind their backs. We feel compelled to respond with generosity and love when an impoverished homeless man asks us for help. We feel compelled to serve in teams at church that seek to engage with and serve deprived parts of the community.

These responses are fantastic! This is God's Holy Spirit at work in us, compelling us so that his kingdom is extended in the world around us. But do you notice what each of these examples is? Each one is a response; it is an example of the way we react in a Christ-like manner in certain situations. If we really want to build God's kingdom, I'm convinced it isn't just about how we *react* in certain situations; we have to think about how we *pro-act* too. It's not just about responding in a Christ-like way when certain opportunities present themselves to us; it's about going out and seeking those opportunities to transform our culture and build God's kingdom on our own initiative. Shunning the Selfish Gospel doesn't just mean being radically sacrificial in our reactions; it means being radically sacrificial in our self-prompted actions.

It's all about actively assessing our lives to work out where the opportunities are for us to work for the restoration of creation. This may appear to be a bit easier for someone who works as a human rights lawyer compared to someone who works as a manufacturer on a production line (with no offence meant to those who work in either of these environments). But if someone works as a human rights lawyer, then they are very obviously acting as an agent for justice every day, whereas if we work on a production line, the opportunities to work for justice and mercy may be more covert. This said, Jesus didn't differentiate, as far as I am aware, between lawyers and labourers. Our identity as children of God is what prompts Jesus' call for us to proactively build his kingdom here on Earth.

Simply *reacting* in a Christ-like way is fantastic, but actually it's not that defining. There are plenty of very nice people in the world who volunteer to help out in their neighbourhoods when the opportunity presents itself, who give money to the poor and who refuse to gossip about their co-workers. Most of the atheists I know are very nice people. If I'm honest, a lot of them are actually much nicer than many Christians I know. Being nice and responding to certain situations in a kindly way is wonderful, but Christ calls us to be more than that – and being more than that is what sets us apart.

To go back to our factory analogy, if we only wait for opportunities to build God's kingdom to present themselves, it's like we're standing in the car park of our factory, waiting for the right raw materials to magically be driven past on the back of a truck. If we spend enough time in the car park, the right materials *may* pass us at some point, but it will take a fair amount of time. However, if we are actively seeking out opportunities to build God's kingdom, then, rather than just standing waiting in the car park, it's as though we're putting orders in with our suppliers, directing them to the factory and making room for them to unload. We're actively seeking out those raw materials and encouraging them to move towards us, and so we're going to get through a lot more kingdom building.

HOW TO BUILD A BASE CAMP

So that's the attitude of shunning the Selfish Gospel, the attitude of kingdom building – but what about the practicalities? How do we actually live in such a way that we're proactively seeking opportunities to transform our environment and build God's kingdom? And in our churches, how can we encourage that as a lifestyle? Two ways spring to mind.

First, we build a culture of church where we are compelled to go out and engage with the community at large, rather than a culture of church in which the community of the church dominates all other aspects of our lives. Second, we enable members of the church to see opportunities to build God's kingdom as they engage with the community at large, and equip them to take those opportunities.

If you want to classify very broadly, there are two ways in which we build God's kingdom in our free (non-work) time. The first is in formalized church activities, often within the church buildings, such as Alpha courses, youth groups, serving church charity initiatives, parenting and marriage courses, and so on. These are courses and activities arranged and run by the church, and generally they go a long way to having an impact on the lives of others with the love of God. If someone without a faith is prepared to attend these courses or be involved with these activities, they are likely really to grow towards God as they participate – even if they don't make a formal commitment of faith.

The second way, broadly speaking, is through investing in informal relationships. This is usually done outside of the church building (though not always). These activities are things like joining or participating in a local sports club, getting involved with a volunteer charity effort, becoming a part of the community at the local pub or just investing in relationships in our place of work. In general, these activities appear to have a subtler kingdom impact – it's much less common to lead someone to faith in Christ over a quiet pint in your local than it is on an Alpha course. However, these activities are no less vital. It is through investing in relationships outside of formal church activities that we are able to go on and invite people to those formal church activities. We could run the best Alpha course in the world, but if no-one in the church has friends who aren't Christians, then no-one will turn up because no-one will be invited!

Therefore, it's important to find a balance between formal church activities and informal activities. Rather than doing our church services on a Sunday, volunteering to serve on the youth team on a Monday, doing home group on a Tuesday, running the Alpha course on a Wednesday, participating in a church prayer meeting on the Thursday and organizing worship group practice on a Friday (leaving Saturday as an exhausted day to spend time with those we love), we need to make time away from church. As members of the church, we need to seriously consider limiting our participation in church activities, maybe spending one or two nights a week doing 'church stuff', plus Sunday services.

Now, my opinion is not prescriptive – I told you at the start of this book that I'm a relatively normal person! But I know that it is important to back up broad ideas with specific suggestions. Therefore, forgive me as I suggest, in an ideal world, that we would spend one night a week investing in a discipling relationship (having a meal or a coffee with either those who are discipling us or those whom we are discipling – possibly rotating between the two on alternate weeks), and one night a week serving the church in a formalized church activity of some kind: helping out with the youth group, or Alpha course, or helping out on a parenting course, for example.

When you consider that many people in the church will then probably spend at least one night a week socializing with people in the church, a couple of nights in the week at home – relaxing with family and so on – and then Sundays in church, that still only leaves one night a week to go out and informally invest in the community outside of the church.

For those who serve in church on a Sunday and need to prepare, such as worship teams, they could combine that preparation with the evening they spend investing in discipling relationships. Being discipled by someone who serves the church in a similar way is a great way of meeting the specific challenges that role brings. For example, the team could spend the first couple of hours of the evening preparing for Sunday, and then perhaps close with an hour of discipleship.

The problem that this model of church brings is a lack of volunteers. As we alluded to in chapter 1, many churches, especially small churches, are reliant on a core of twenty-five to fifty volunteers who attend and run almost everything that the church does. If those twenty-five volunteers are told to help out at just one thing each per week, then the operating capacity of the church is hugely reduced.

That is why it is essential that we understand the full breadth of the gospel and grasp the importance of God's kingdom – especially our role as disciples in building it. Church doesn't work if we as the body do not all realize the role we have to play.

It's only if we are effectively taught that church is about building God's kingdom – that this is the purpose that we were saved for and is an essential part of the gospel – that our churches then grasp the need to go out and do it. Because then, rather than having a small number of committed volunteers, our entire church is a team of committed volunteers. Everyone grasps the essential nature of building God's kingdom and is prepared to contribute, both in formalized church activities and in less formal engagement with the community outside of the church.

And again, personal transformation is also essential to this model of church. We need to be growing in Christ personally if we hope to share him with others. There's no point in committing to attend the local pub quiz every week to invest in relationships there if we aren't going to be growing in Jesus and demonstrating his king-dom to those at the pub. We need to be mindful of our role as kingdom builders and growing in that role through personal discipleship if we hope to be effective.

ENVISIONING AND EQUIPPING THE MOUNTAIN CLIMBERS

So once we've equipped people to go out and engage with their communities, what happens next? Regardless of where we are, we can arguably start with a simple question: 'What would it look like if God's kingdom was accomplished in this place?' We ask God to show us what it would look like if his perfect will were accomplished in the situation we find ourselves in, whether that is a work environment, the local neighbourhood or the town in which we live.

This is not a question we can answer lightly; it takes time and patience; shunning the Selfish Gospel and spending ourselves in carefully seeking God's voice over a period of months, if not years. It's often not a question we can answer immediately as we begin a journey of discipleship; it takes time and spiritual maturity to get into God's rhythm and understand his will in certain situations. But as we grow in God through discipleship and press him with this question, he gradually reveals a vision for our situation.

Once we have that vision, we ask ourselves a second question: 'What can I do to move that vision closer to accomplishment?' We have to assess our skills, our areas of influence and the unique opportunities that we have been given. Again, this is a process that takes time. We really need to know ourselves and be comfortable honestly assessing our skills and abilities. It requires a certain level of spiritual maturity on our behalf.

But once we have answered both of the above questions, we can marry the two answers: we find the sweet spot where our skills and opportunities are being used to build the vision of God's kingdom that he has given us for our local area. We find that place where we can serve God and proactively work for love, mercy and justice in the situations in which we find ourselves. If we view our outward-looking mission to see the kingdom of God in terms of restoring 'right relationships' with God, within ourselves, with each other and with the environment, it can help us really grasp the vision and opportunity to grow any or all four aspects in the outside-of-church environment in which we find ourselves.

CONCLUSION

We have previously seen that some parts of the church are suffering from collective locked-in syndrome, struggling to interact well with the outside world. Now, we have explored some of the various ways in which we can seek to build God's kingdom as a church. It always starts with personal transformation – growing God's kingdom inside ourselves through discipleship. Then, to build God's kingdom around us, we need an outward-looking attitude, where we are actively encouraged to spend time away from the church investing in relationships with those who aren't Christians. We also need to install outward-looking ways into our lives in practice as we seek to build God's kingdom throughout our communities.

9 The cure
Rehabilitating the Elephant Man

PREACHING TO THE MED STUDENT MASSES

I stood there nervously, feeling like I might melt from the intensity of their gazes at any second. I remember feeling quite certain that no-one who'd heard what I'd just said was ever going to speak to me again. I also worried that the assessor might fail me for being too controversial!

I was in my fifth year of medical school and we were doing a week-long course on 'Teaching Skills'. The logic behind it was that every doctor is in many ways a teacher, and so we should learn some proper techniques for teaching. As part of the course we had been split into groups of eight or ten people and asked to perform a 'micro-teach' session, where we each spent around eight minutes teaching the group a new skill. Most people opted to demonstrate how to make origami or how to tie a bow-tie. I however, had decided to teach people why they should keep an open mind, particularly in regard to faith.

Some of the bolder evangelists reading this may be thinking, 'Great idea! Easy!' For me, however, this was another big 'gulp' moment. I was at Imperial College for medical school – a science and technology college well known for being very scientifically orientated. Now, some of the finest Christians I know are scientists. But there also seems to be a tendency among some of my scientific colleagues towards a particularly aggressive brand of atheism – with some people being quite hostile and contemptuous towards those with a faith. This brand of atheism tends to overstate the value of science as being the only source of useful or 'worthy' knowledge and treats faith as something that shouldn't be trusted.

So when it was my turn to do this 'micro-teach', I got up and asked the group a question. 'What scientific evidence is there that last week happened and that it happened how we remember it?' Put another way, how can we prove that last week proceeded as we recall with the help of science?' No-one came up with anything. Eventually someone suggested news and media pieces. In reply, I pointed out to them that news articles or media pieces are not scientific evidence. Scientific evidence is evidence gained from experimentation in order to prove a hypothesis, and importantly it is reproducible, meaning that if the experiment is repeated again and again, the same outcome would occur. News articles and media pieces are records of historical evidence.

I pointed this out to the group, and explained there is no scientific evidence for history – that's not how science works – and therefore, although we are all heavily wedded to scientific knowledge as the 'best knowledge', in some situations it's not the most important type of knowledge. For instance, when it comes to history we are reliant on historical knowledge (like news articles and media pieces). I demonstrated how little knowledge each of us has compared to all of the knowledge in the world that humanity has ever possessed, and I concluded by suggesting that because none of us has all of the knowledge, it's very hard to state categorically that faith is without an evidence base, and therefore we should all keep an open mind rather than definitively closing ourselves off to the idea of faith. Cue the flurry of intense stares.

Some people in the group were very good friends, and some were casual acquaintances. For others in the group, this was the first conversation I had ever had with them. But nobody really responded positively to what I had had to say. Needless to say, I was the Elephant Man in the room.

For me, this example is illustrative of the reception our faith often receives in our society. In that situation, I wasn't even talking about my faith – I didn't mention Jesus once! I just had to mention the idea that we might not want to rule faith out completely, and it seemed to turn the whole group against what I was saying.

Our acceptance of the Selfish Gospel and failure to embrace the kingdom of God and understand our role in it has specifically led to the church's Elephant Man syndrome. Our delirious discipleship and inward-looking nature mean we are failing to transform into the likeness of Christ, and without this transformation, many areas of the church are too often seen as irrelevant or even unattractive by the rest of society. But once again, we see that Jesus' instructions about the kingdom of God provide the only treatment we will ever need.

A SHINING EXAMPLE FOR ALL ETERNITY

Have you ever heard of LIV village? It's a village in South Africa founded and run by Tich and Joan Smith. These amazing, godly people were both saved by God's grace from the most devastating social circumstances. Having saved them, he set them to work building his kingdom. He sent them to a township in Durban, South Africa, called Amaoti. This is the largest slum settlement in Durban and it is an area that is in desperate need of God's kingdom. They worked in this area for years, building relationships with the community and running feeding and educational programmes for those in need.

God was so delighted with the work Tich and Joan were doing that he gave them more to do. He gave Tich a vision of a village on a hill that would be for orphans in the area. Here these orphans would live in homes with a foster mother who would love them as a birth mother; they would receive a good education and a safe space to live in. More than any of that, they would receive spiritual discipline and would grow up strong in the Lord. Local people would be employed in the village; it would strive to be self-sustaining and community friendly. Above all, the village would be a manifestation of God's mercy and grace poured out for the lost and the broken. In 2008 this village became a reality, and it has gone from strength to strength ever since.

The village works on the mantra that its people rescue a child, restore a life, raise up a leader and release a star. It is an incredible example of God's will in action, taking the broken and restoring it to wholeness. Tich and Joan Smith are transformed people who are transforming lives for the glory of God. If you want to read their story, they have a fantastic book called *When Grace Showed Up*.[22]

In Ephesians 3:10, Paul states that God's plan is that 'now, through the church, the manifold wisdom of God should be made known to the rulers and authorities in the heavenly realms'.

By that, Paul meant that God intended the church to be so beautiful, its example so shining, that it would stand as a testament to his incredible wisdom in pouring out his mercy and saving grace in the person of Jesus. This testament is not just meant to stand for the people of Earth; the church's example is meant to be so incredible that it shines forth *beyond* space and time.

That's the church! The random collection of assorted humans who we meet with on a Sunday morning are meant to be that example – living out God's glory in such a demonstrable way that we shine beyond the universe, for all eternity. Sometimes, particularly when I reflect on my own life, I find that hard to grasp. But when you see Christians like Tich and Joan Smith, and hear about things like LIV village, God's perfect wisdom in choosing the church as his example for all eternity becomes so clear. When you see the faces of the children who live there and hear their stories of transform-ation, you really can taste God's kingdom in the most beautiful way.

I truly believe that the kind of work that Tich and Joan Smith are doing is not meant for the privileged few 'celebrity' Christians. This faith is not about a 'Holy Elite'. We are all members of the same church, and we are all called to be that same shining example. God has a plan to transform and grow each and every one of us, and he has kingdom-building work for each and every one of us to do.

The vast majority of us won't be called to leave our lives behind and go and work in a slum in South Africa, but that doesn't mean that we can neglect personal transformation or the growth of God's kingdom where we are either. As we now look at how we can rehabilitate the Elephant Man church and cure our pariah-like status, we're going to consider what it would mean for us if we were to be this shining example that Paul calls us to.

We're going to look at each of the issues we raised in chapter 3 in turn: first, we're going to think about our isolation and cultural distinction from the world; next we're going to think about how we relate to a culture that is not comfortable with the concept of personal 'sin' and doesn't feel in need of a saviour; and finally we're going to think about the bad PR we've suffered over the past few years and the increasing distrust of big institutions.

CULTURALLY DISTINCT?

Way back in the 'diagnosis', we looked at how Jesus calls us to be a part of the world but to remain culturally distinct from it: living by his values instead of the values of the world. What I suggested is that too often we are living by values that are similar to the rest of our culture (some of us just Christianize them before we adopt them), but despite this we are inhabiting a subculture, isolating ourselves from the mainstream by building a Christian bubble.

If we were to grasp a broad gospel and engage with the kingdom-building work that it entails, then our situation would be radically different. We have seen previously in the 'cure' how the true response to a full gospel has to be one of personal transformation, and if we were each transformed by the gospel, then we wouldn't be holding on to Christianized versions of the values our culture holds dear. Instead, we would be holding on to God's values as we are transformed into his likeness by the power of his Holy Spirit.

Individualism would be dethroned as we understand Jesus' call to live lives of sacrificial love. Consumerism would be knocked out as we grow into lives that are perfectly satisfied with God's awesome providence. Each of us would enjoy life in all its fullness through relationship with Jesus. If we lived by that template, growing in and being perfected by God's unending love, we would be holding radically different values and dreams from those of our society.

In the same way, we have seen how a broad gospel calls us to build God's kingdom in the world around us. This effort is only truly possible if we are engaged with the world around ourselves, outside of our Christian subculture, in a real and vulnerable way. God's kingdom is poured out in sacrificial love – it is only complete in its vulnerability. God's kingdom on Earth, by its very nature, cannot remain apart from the brokenness it is surrounded by. And so, as we grow in Christ and let the Holy Spirit use us, we find that he compels us to be open and vulnerable with the communities outside of our church. Jesus wants us to have real, deep friendship with those people outside of our Christianese bubble.

In this way, as we let the Holy Spirit build God's kingdom both in us and in the world through us, we would grow in our connection with the world while also becoming more culturally distinct from it. And I truly believe it's as we have those real connections and vulnerable friendships with people outside of our churches, while also holding radically different values from them, that we are best positioned to be a shining example of Christ's beauty.

SIN REALIZED?

It's also in that place that I think we are best positioned to act as a mirror to the world itself.

Nobody likes someone who sits on an imagined pedestal and hands out unwanted advice. Being a know-it-all is never an attractive quality. The danger for us as a church, with our culture that is so blind to 'sin', is that we come across like that. If we were to spend our lives pointing our fingers at people, acting as if we are holier than everyone else and generally explaining to people how broken they are, then they would not respond positively. That style of advice is, in my opinion, only ever really appropriate if we have a close, pre-existing relationship with someone (unless they explicitly ask for the advice, of course!). But that then forces us to ask the question: how is our culture ever going to realize its need for a saviour if it continues to be oblivious to its sin and doesn't invite us to warn it? The answer is that we need to act like a mirror to the world.

The idea of God's kingdom, displayed through the people of the church, is that our example is so beautiful, radical and holy that to look upon us makes you realize the brokenness you're living in.

Think of it like this. My bedroom light is quite dull and although it doesn't cause too many problems, when I'm getting ready in the evenings this dull light makes all of my clothes look clean. I can give my clothes a quick smell-check, put them on and head out for the night. Except, when I reach my destination, the usually far brighter lights have an unfortunate habit of showing up all these stains and dirty marks on my clothes that I couldn't see in my bedroom. It really is quite embarrassing!

We as the church are meant to be like those bright lights. When people are in the midst of their normal lives, their clothes may look clean. But, when they meet someone from the church, someone who is living in God's kingdom, the light is supposed to be so bright that it shows up all these dirty marks and stains that we didn't even realize we had. It's not that we should be holding spotlights, pointing them at those dirty marks; it's that our very presence is supposed to carry the holy scent of God. Being around a Christian is meant to be like tasting heaven – and when people look at themselves in the light of that flavour, they have a realization of their brokenness.

Now, that only works if we're in regular, real contact with people who aren't members of the church. We can't have that impact if we only ever socialize with Christians. Have you ever tried to use a torch in a bright room? It just doesn't work; there's simply too much background light for your torch to make any impact. In the same way, we can be as holy as we like in church (and I would encourage us all to do that!) but actually, our holiness will only make a significant impact in the world if we are living among people who don't already have an understanding of that holiness.

I don't think this is an abstract idea. Our culture is full of 'clicktivists' rather than 'activists'. By that, I mean that as a generation so many of us hold beautiful, righteous values of peace and justice for the poor – Christian and non-Christian alike. And we're all prepared to stand up for those values … but only when we don't have to put much effort into it.

We're all very keen to sign petitions, post encouraging Facebook statuses and tweet about things that are wrong with the world. But we're not so great at sustained, persistent effort. A few of us might go on a day-long protest over issues we feel especially passionate about – but how many of us are prepared to really inconvenience ourselves in a sustained way to stand up for a serious issue? When I look at myself and my friends, I'm not sure how many of us are.

The mantra of our culture sometimes seems to be that we will support any good cause, as long as it doesn't cost us too much. The click of a mouse, a few seconds to type a tweet – even a day out to protest in central London – we can do that. But we're not always so good at supporting these causes when it really costs. We're not always so great when the sacrifice starts to hurt.

For us as a church, this presents us with an amazing opportunity. As we've explored throughout this book, Jesus calls us to pay the cost and make that kind of sacrifice every day. He calls us to walk the walk as well as talk the talk, not just when it suits us, not only when we can afford it, but every day.

If we can live out that example, if we can demonstrate that kind of willingness to sacrifice on behalf of others regularly, then that is an amazing statement to make. What a fantastic example of the gospel that would be.

GOOD PR?

When I first went to medical school, my dad (who is also a doctor) gave me some advice that will stay with me for ever. He said:

'Freddie, a patient will forgive you anything if you are kind to them. You could make a mistake, even miss the most serious diagnosis, but if you are kind to them and if they know you and understand that you care for them, then they will forgive you. If you're mean, then they won't forgive you anything.'

My dad's advice was quite simple. In medicine, relationship is key. Having a relationship with your patients is vital because the truth is that everybody makes mistakes. If you want to have any hope of being forgiven when you make those mistakes, then you need to make sure that you have invested in relationship with your patients first.

In some ways I think the problem is, as a church, we have too often dismissed this advice. Too often we have made mistakes and been able to hide behind our privileged status as part of the wider establishment. If we truly want people's forgiveness when we mess up, we need to have real, vulnerable relationships with them.

Sadly, I don't think any organization run by real people can avoid those mistakes. To mess up is to be human. And although I don't think anyone can demand forgiveness, if we are in a position where we are actively loving people as a real part of their community, then I think we are much more likely to receive it.

The other great thing about being a real part of our community is that we are much better positioned to draw attention to the amazing good that the church is already doing. A relatively recent survey found that the church provides up to 1.4 million volunteers every year who take part in church-based projects. Combined, they put in in 115 million man-hours, which are worth an estimated £2.4 billion to our society.[23] That is good news: the gospel in action!

For many (certainly in my experience), the example of these volunteers is not seen as 'normal' for Christians that they know. People pigeonhole these efforts to the work of a few kind souls who perhaps have nothing better to do, and by doing so they distance the efforts of these volunteers from a radical gospel message. It allows many in our society to hear these statistics while maintaining the belief that the church is full of naïve, boring people wearing socks with sandals. It allows them to dismiss our message as something that is irrelevant for our culture.

If we rose up as a generation and ensured that we were a real part of the communities outside of our churches then, without saying a word, those amazing volunteer hours would speak volumes. Not only would people hear those statistics; they would have a real friendship with someone who is engaged in that work and who they already know is a beautiful, shining example of God's kingdom. They would have a face to put to an otherwise faceless statistic – and in doing that, they would become more aware of the beautiful work that the church is already doing.

IT'S ALL ABOUT RELATIONSHIP

When it comes to rehabilitating the Elephant Man-like church, I think the key is relationship. It is very easy to criticize those that we don't know, but a real relationship offers a real understanding. If we are engaging with those outside of our church communities in a real and vulnerable way, this will inevitably begin to bridge the gap between the church and the outside world. Our atheist and agnostic friends might not believe what we believe, but at least this clear communication will enable them to know where we are coming from. It's when we have those real connections with people that the kingdom of God can start to shine through our lives. And it's when people are seeing the kingdom of God and not a load of broken Christians that the church–Elephant Man will be rehabilitated.

CONCLUSION

The church is called to be a shining example of God's will that stands testament to his glory throughout space and time. It is as the Holy Spirit transforms us into that example, by building his kingdom in our hearts and using us to build his kingdom in the world, that we will see rehabilitation of our Elephant Man status.

As we are transformed in this way, we will become distinct from culture while at the same time being compelled to be involved in it in a way that is vulnerable and real. It's also in that place that we will be able to act as a mirror to our society, that they can look upon us and come to a realization of their brokenness – in a way that isn't judgmental or rude. Finally, it is as we are transformed into that shining example that we will be able to rehabilitate our public image and restore trust in the church body as a whole. At its heart, the key is for us to rebuild relationships with our communities and those who aren't yet in touch with the church, because it is when we are connected to people in a real and vulnerable way that the kingdom of God can start to shine into their lives, and they will grasp the true beauty of the church.

Concluding remarks

A recent survey found that three million people regularly attend church in the UK, which is around 6.3% of the total population.[24] That's around the same size as the US Department of Defense (the world's largest employer) or 50% bigger than the staff of Walmart (who also own Asda supermarkets). So actually that means there are as many regular attenders of church in the UK as there are employees at the largest organization on the planet – and that's just Christians in the UK. According to official statistics, at the time of writing there are 2.2 billion Christians in the world (31% of the population).[25]

As we have examined throughout this book, our culture is broken and in need of sacrificial love. Although we may not confess our need for a saviour, our culture is crying out for committed, real relationship with the Creator of Relationships. We need the kingdom of God to be present in this nation more than ever.

As a church, both in the UK and globally, we are a hugely powerful group. We are able to have an immense impact on our society and our culture, to show them that love and to build that kingdom. All we need is to act together and speak with one transformed voice – and we would see the nation transformed.

I don't think that's as far-fetched as it may sound. It isn't beyond us! It all begins with shunning the Selfish Gospel and embracing our fresh understanding of Jesus' gospel in its entirety. It begins with grasping the role of God's kingdom in the gospel and in our personal journey of faith. As we understand that our gospel calls for us to be transformed – to submit to the Holy Spirit as he builds his kingdom in our hearts – we start to engage with it.

That process of kingdom building starts with a process of discipleship: personal transformation towards Christ's likeness, allowing him to build his kingdom in our hearts so that we are changed. As we grow in that kingdom and are changed personally, it starts to spill out of us. We naturally become more peaceful, more loving, more generous, more kind. But more than that, we also become intentional about those values. We start looking for ways to build the kingdom in our society. We start looking for opportunities to restore people to right relationship with God, to right relationship with themselves, to right relationship with each other and to right relationship with the environment.

As we become agents of that transformation, working for restoration and reconciliation everywhere we go, Christians throughout the UK and beyond will become known as people who are prepared to go the extra mile. We would be known as people who are prepared to sacrifice for others, people who will give themselves to bring peace and hope to a situation.

I firmly believe that as those expressions of Christianity that are struggling to have a transformative influence grasp the true nature of God's kingdom and understand the purpose it gives us, our nation will be transformed. As we grow into transformed people who are intent on transforming the world, our culture will sit up and take note. Our faith will once again be as powerful, healthy and alive as it has ever been.

The key to having that impact, though, is not a national strategy or a global initiative. Instead, it starts with you and me. Little by little, as each of us is transformed, the impact will spread and grow. If we want to transform the nation, we have to start by letting Christ transform ourselves. When we know the glorious wholeness and endless possibilities found in Christ and our role in building his kingdom here on Earth, why would we settle for less? Why would we settle for the Selfish Gospel? Why would we not give it all?

The Jesus Gospel

- ☑ Loved?
- ☑ Forgiven?
- ☑ Builder of God's Kingdom?

Notes

1 <www.telegraph.co.uk/news/religion/12095251/Church-of-England-attendance-plunges-to-record-low.html>
2 <www.brierleyconsultancy.com/capitalgrowth>
3 <www.churchofengland.org/media-centre/news/2014/01/signs-of-growth.aspx>
4 Mike Breen, *Building a Discipling Culture* (Kairos, 2009).
5 A. W. Tozer, *The Pursuit of God* (Christian Publications, 1948).
6 Richard Foster, *A Celebration of Discipline* (Hodder & Stoughton, 2008).
7 Foster, *Celebration of Discipline*, p. 8.
8 Breen, *Discipling Culture*, p. 29.
9 <www.telegraph.co.uk/news/religion/12095251/Church-of-England-attendance-plunges-to-record-low.html>
10 <www.christian.org.uk/ashers-baking-company>
11 <www.theguardian.com/society/2009/jul/22/weston-super-mare-rehab-regulation>
12 <www.nouvelles.umontreal.ca/udem-news/news/20091201-are-the-effects-of pornography-negligible.html>
13 Tom Wright, *Surprised by Hope: Rethinking Heaven, the Resurrection and the Mission of the Church* (HarperOne, 2008), p. 19.
14 Ronald Sider, *The Scandal of the Evangelical Conscience* (Baker, 2005), p. 59.

15 Amy Sherman, *Kingdom Calling* (IVP, 2012).

16 See above, n. 5.

17 See above, n. 6.

18 See above, n. 4.

19 <www.livelife123.org>

20 Kris Vallotton, *How Heaven Invades Earth* (Regal, 2010).

21 See above, n. 15.

22 Tich and Joan Smith with Liza Hoeksma, *When Grace Showed Up* (David C. Cook, 2016).

23 <www.churchtimes.co.uk/articles/2015/13-march/news/uk/ increase-in-church-based-volunteering>

24 <www.eauk.org/church/research-and-statistics/english-church- census.cfm>

25 <www.pewforum.org/2011/12/19/global-christianity-exec>